SEE JOHNNY READ!

SEE JOHNNY READ!

The 5 Most Effective Ways to End Your Son's Reading Problems

Tracey Wood

McGraw-Hill

New York   Chicago   San Francisco   Lisbon   London
Madrid   Mexico City   Milan   New Delhi   San Juan
Seoul   Singapore   Sydney   Toronto

*The **McGraw·Hill** Companies*

1 2 3 4 5 6 7 8 9 0 AGM/AGM 0 9 8 7 6 5 4 3

ISBN 0-07-141721-4

McGraw-Hill books are available at special quantity discounts to use as premiums and sales promotions, or for use in corporate training programs. For more information, please write to the Director of Special Sales, Professional Publishing, McGraw-Hill, Two Penn Plaza, New York, NY 10121-2298. Or contact your local bookstore.

 This book is printed on recycled, acid-free paper containing a minimum of symbol 50% recycled, de-inked fiber.

For Wayne, Bradley, Anthony, Ricky, Tim,
and all the irrepressible and wonderful boys
who taught me and continue to teach me

Contents

Acknowledgments

For endless help, feedback, and time to work when I should've been doing mom things, thank you to my wonderful husband and children.

Thanks to my mom, Gillian Hirst. When I was a child, she took me to the local library on Friday evenings, rain or shine. Thanks to my stepdad, Frank Hirst; he helped me all through my college years. To the good friends and colleagues who encouraged me, read for me, and shared their stories, thanks so much: Julie Burke, Andelys Jolley, Marian Stoney, Carolyn Thompson, Bonnie Velcich, Colleen Devlin, Paul Besant, Frances Faflik, Vandy Shrader, and Laura Browne.

And finally, thanks to those who sharpened my vision: Dr. J. S. Parnes (San Mateo County Office of Education), Nola Firth (Australian Resource Educators Association), Dr. Susan Miller (University of Nevada), and, of course, my editors, Betsy Lane, Andrew Littell, and Barbara Gilson.

Introduction

When does a reading delay become a reading problem? Is reading harder for boys? What kind of help works best for boys?

For years we've known the worst about boys and reading:

- Boys score lower on reading tests.
- Struggling boys act up in class.
- Half the young adults involved with crime and drugs (mostly boys) can't read well.

Now, thanks to recent national studies, we know more about helping our boys. We know their nature makes learning to read hard for them (they love movement, winning, action); a parent's help counts; struggling boys who get systematic help with phonics and guided reading catch up. We know the early years of school are the best time to help, but, with consistent help, older boys can catch up too.

This book puts information from educational studies into simple, step-by-step, practical terms. It shows how we can help our sons best, in school and out.

SEE JOHNNY READ!

PART 1

The First Way:
Break through
the "Wait a While"
Barrier

*W*hen your son struggles with reading, you nearly always hear the words "wait a while." Don't. Without early intervention, reading difficulties get worse.

CHAPTER 1

Does Johnny Have a Problem?

A PASSING PHASE OR A LASTING PROBLEM?

When Johnny seems to be falling behind in reading, we ask questions:

- Is he just a late developer?
- How far behind must he be before we worry?
- Will his difficulties last?

Should We Wait for Johnny to Mature?

With reading, we can't afford to "wait a while." There's a window of opportunity for Johnny to learn to read, and if we act too late, it's closed.

Warning: Johnny Has a Problem If He's Not Beginning to Read at 6 or 7 Years Old

If, when Johnny is 5, a teacher says he's not developmentally ready to read and will catch up later, she may be perfectly right. Allow Johnny time to mature. If a teacher says the same when Johnny is 7, don't wait.

Real Life: Harry, Lucky at 7

Harry was 7 years old and in grade 1 at a regular public school. He was struggling with reading and was unable to read the beginners' books sent home with him each week. He was starting to resent being cajoled and helped by his mom, Sheila. Sheila, growing weary and concerned, wanted to have Harry privately tutored. His classroom teacher, who was also the vice principal of the school, didn't agree with Harry being tutored. He accepted that Harry was surprisingly slow in beginning to read, but was not convinced this justified private tutoring. He advised Harry's mom to wait a while, to give Harry time to mature. Weeks went by, and still Harry was unable to read his books, although his teacher spent time each day helping him. Harry became more reluctant to read books at home, and Sheila contacted me.

Sheila told me she was worried sick. She could see Harry was performing at a lower level than his older sister had at the same age; he was much weaker than friends and cousins of the same age. Would he really improve if she gave him time to mature? I asked Sheila if she felt Harry would benefit from waiting. She didn't. She wanted to act, not wait, so I started tutoring Harry. You can read about the SPRint program I used in Chapter 6, but the main point of Harry's case is that after just 20 lessons he was read-ing basic books. Better still, he was enjoying it, and Sheila felt a weight lifted from her shoulders.

Why was Harry so successful? Because he got the best possible help, good one-on-one tutoring, at the best possible age, 7 years old.

Real Life: Help Came Late to Alex, Aged 10

Alex was 10 and very cool. He wore earrings and a hairstyle that required careful spiking with lots of hair gel. He didn't want to be tutored. His mom warned me that tutoring might not work for Alex, he might not agree to it. I was prepared for tough things.

When I first spoke to Alex, he tried to maintain disinterest. He didn't face me at all for the first few minutes, but I doggedly stated my case: I wanted to help; I knew he felt angry at being treated like he was "dumb"; I had worked with many kids who felt just like him and knew all about hard and boring lessons. My work was going to help him, and I promised it would be fun.

Alex, as it turned out, was a dream student. He loved to hear all about other cool boys or boys who had been in trouble, and thought our sessions were "way cool." He always came to our lessons, completed all the homework I gave, and made steady progress. His mom, Jennifer, was thrilled. But Alex had to work on his reading for a whole school year, and it was hard on his ego. Not only do children older than 9 catch up more slowly, but their attitudes are different. It was difficult for Alex to accept help: Work had to seem mature yet not too hard, and to top it off he had his fragile adolescent dignity to preserve.

Age Facts

- With intensive reading instruction, 95 percent of struggling children under the age of 10 catch up.
- If Johnny is 10 or older, we must really commit ourselves to helping because catching up is harder for him. Only 25 percent of struggling children aged 10 and older catch up.
- It takes four times as long to teach a fourth-grade child to read as it does to teach a kindergartner.

Will Johnny's Problems Last?

The simple answer to this question is that good teachers (and tutors) make the difference. The single most important influence on Johnny's success in class will be his teacher.

What can we do to help? We can learn to spot good teachers and influence (for the better!) the not-so-good teachers.

Real Life: How to Spot a Good Teacher

When I met Danny, aged 7, he was reading well below his age level and struggled with three-letter words. His mother said that Danny's teacher, Mr. Greeve, did wonders with the resources he had. Unfortunately, Mr. Greeve's time was stretched, and Danny needed more help than Mr. Greeve could possibly give. I started to tutor Danny and arranged to meet Mr. Greeve. I hoped Mr. Greeve would help me by complementing the work I did with Danny. I knew if we could coordinate our efforts, Danny would benefit. I went to Danny's school optimistically.

When I arrived, long before the start of the school day, the building was quiet. I wandered around and found the principal. I explained that I had come to meet Mr. Greeve, and was offered coffee and a seat in the staff room. A great start! Mr. Greeve entered. He wore a tracksuit and was carrying an impressive collection of books and general teaching paraphernalia. He was an older man, but appeared youthful. Lively and engaging, he was a person with plenty to do and say. He balanced his own coffee in a free hand and led the way to his classroom. Predictably enough, Mr. Greeve's classroom was busy and cheerful, just like him.

Mr. Greeve was something of a realist. He told me he had too many students, not enough time, and inadequate resources. He lamented that he had other students whose problems were even worse than Danny's. But, he said, one afternoon every week, with help from another teacher, he split the class and tried to fast-track literacy skills with the weaker students. This, he said, was the best he could do. That, I thought, was probably better than many teachers did with all the resources in the world.

Without pretense or ceremony, Mr. Greeve focused on practical solutions. For the rest of the school year, Mr. Greeve and I pooled our knowledge and efforts. We worked on sequential phonics skills, spelling rules, and lots of reading at Danny's level. Danny reaped the benefits of having two professionals join forces on his behalf. His work was never too difficult, he was never without support, and he learned to read. Perhaps even more important, he was happy and confident.

Good Teachers

Good teachers make experiences lively, allow children movement breaks to help them concentrate, protect each child's self-esteem, and modify work for weak readers. They are flexible and willing to consider change.

Movement Is Especially Important for Boys

All of us need movement, of course, but some of us, especially boys, need more! We are the knee jigglers, finger tappers, and general fidgeters, and we can't concentrate fully without moving a little. Occupational therapists are familiar with this and often provide restless children with devices to use in class. Among the gadgets I've seen are small toys to squeeze, special cushions to wriggle on, and shaped pencils that feel far nicer than our usual skinny ones!

Bad Teaching

Not all of our sons can get the great teachers. Some of us will feel unhappy about the person who spends most of every day with our son. So what does bad, or at least less than great, teaching look like? The following comments are typical of the things parents say to me:

"Every time I asked about Steven, the teacher said he was doing OK."

"Wayne was always in trouble with the teacher. It got so he cried every morning because he didn't want to go to class."

"The teacher used to shout at Daniel in front of the others, Daniel felt all the kids were laughing at him."

"Richard started to act up because he just couldn't understand what was going on."

"I told Adam's teacher he couldn't read, but the teacher never modified anything for him; he brought homework back and couldn't even read the instructions, let alone do the work."

"I tell Mrs. McNally how hard it is for Joe, but nothing changes, and Joe says she gives him a hard time if I go in, he doesn't want me to go in again."

"Mr. Carter told me he has 30 kids in his class and 10 of them need extra help, most of the 10 are worse off than Tyler."

"Jason's teacher said there just aren't the resources."

Bad Things Teachers Say

When I was a schoolteacher, especially at high school, I heard plenty of not so tolerant or understanding comments from teachers. Their heavy workload made them frosty, and their experiences with kids with reading difficulties were brief and uncomfortable:

"He's a pain; his brother was just the same."

"They think they can do what they want these days."

"He wastes everybody's time."

"His mom's too soft with him; he needs a good spanking."

"He's just lazy."

"He's a troublemaker."

"He ought to realize it's not easy for anyone; he's not the only one."

"If he paid more attention, he'd be able to do the work."
"If we got all these time wasters out of school, the bright
ones would have a better chance."
"I've got 27 other kids; I'm not preparing special work for him."

"Bad" Sounds Harsh

The word "bad" sounds harsh, but relates to a teacher's
actions. To humiliate, threaten, or disadvantage Johnny is
certainly being a bad teacher. With our vulnerable children in their charge, teachers must constantly appraise
what they do. Luckily, they can easily bring bad teaching
back to great teaching by focusing on simple, practical
ways to accommodate Johnny's needs.

What to Do If Johnny Gets a Weak Teacher

At this point, you're probably feeling uneasy. Can it all be that
bad? Help! Give me something to do, now! Well, don't rush out
to hammer on Johnny's classroom door yet. It's not all like this,
and if it's bad for you now, it won't stay that way (especially after
you've read this book). Vast armies of terrible teachers aren't sit-
ting in wait for our sons, and the few teachers who are jaded or
frustrated, or are simply having a few bad days, can be sweetened.
Be nice to Johnny's teacher. Even if you want to rail about her
insensitivity or lack of effort, don't. Be sweet-tempered and generous. Then, when you're firmly in credit with all things good,
you can make your suggestions. Suggest that the teacher modify work for Johnny. Show how eager you are to help, in class
and at home. Thank the teacher for every little attention or work
adjustment she makes. Like everyone else, Johnny's teacher is
a sucker for praise and attention. She's more likely to be moved
by sweeteners than by the sledgehammer tactic that first springs
to mind!

Getting On the Right Side of Johnny's Teacher

Being friendly with Johnny's teacher and giving her pointers and ideas will be quicker, easier, and probably more effective than getting into a battle with her. Exhaust this possibility before going into combat.

The Teacher Who Won't Give a Direct Answer

What if Johnny's teacher isn't exactly bad or negligent, but doesn't give you answers? You want to know if Johnny's keeping up with peers, but his teacher only tells you things like:

> "Johnny's always cooperative and often does special jobs for me."
>
> "Johnny's learning about the different contexts and uses of language."

This teacher really doesn't want to tell you how Johnny compares with classmates. She won't say whether Johnny's below average and by how much because she's fearful of saying the wrong thing. She doesn't want to cause offense or say something that might be held against her later. You might claim she said Johnny was doing badly when in fact he suffers from dysgraphia, and she should've spotted this! Perhaps you'll go straight to the principal and threaten to take Johnny out of school. The teacher envisages blame and an avalanche of letters and meetings. Of course she's wary! So don't be surprised if the teacher refers you to the principal or requests a later meeting. If this happens, plan for the next meeting to make sure things get done and not just talked about. (See Chapter 4, "Parent-Teacher Conferences.")

You Can't Agree with Johnny's Teacher; What Now?

What if Johnny's teacher disagrees with you and doesn't think you should worry about Johnny? Ask about extra support outside of regular class. Is there a reading or tutoring program Johnny can be included in? Is there a homework club? Are there parent volunteers who could help? Can a teacher show you how to help? If you have the time, you could start a tutoring club yourself where kids are tutored in school, or a "Parents as Tutors" club where parents are taught to tutor their own child at home. It sounds huge but parents have started all sorts of clubs in schools, and tutoring clubs are among the best and most needed. Join or contact the PTA because strong PTAs fund extra programs and extra teachers, and PTA parents know exactly how things work.

The PTA (Parent-Teacher Association) Can Be Scary!

Your first PTA meeting, full of mysterious facts and figures and driven-looking moms, can make you feel like bolting! Try to target one or two individuals. Ask them about themselves. Find an easy job you can do right away, perhaps serving coffee at a fair or helping with hot lunches. Then you'll be committed (so you can't bolt!), and you can learn the complicated things at a slower pace.

IN SHORT

- The window of opportunity for reading is between ages 5 and 7.
- Up to age 10, it's still relatively easy for Johnny to catch up.
- After age 10, Johnny must work harder and for a longer time if he's to catch up, since only 25 percent of kids like him succeed.
- A strong PTA can lobby, and pay, for reading programs and reading teachers in school.

CHAPTER 2

Focusing on Practical Help

GETTING PRACTICAL HELP IS MORE URGENT THAN GETTING MANY OPINIONS

It sounds crazy, but sometimes we hit the "wait a while" barrier by doing too much. We get entrenched in testing, checking out different programs, and consulting with various specialists, and this takes months. All the while, Johnny's passing through different hands but isn't getting practical help. It's important to realize that whatever we call Johnny's difficulties, the main thing he needs is practical help, quickly. Research is clear about what works best for struggling kids, and it's structured teaching in phonics and guided reading in the early years of school.

BUT COULD JOHNNY HAVE A LEARNING DISABILITY?

Under federal law, there are currently 13 official categories of disability, and Specific Learning Disability (SLD) is one of them. If Johnny is generally fine, but struggles with reading, he might fit the SLD category, but to determine whether he does, he must be tested.

Asking for Assessment at School

If you lodge a written request for assessment for SLD, your school district must respond. Give a letter (or the required form) to the principal or send it to the district office. Your referral letter goes to the district, then back to a designated team or individual at Johnny's school. Some team names you might hear include SST (Student Study Team), CST (Child Study Team), and IAT (Intervention Assistance Team).

Once the team has received your written referral, it must write an IAP (Individual Assessment Plan) within 15 days. Now you meet with the team, and it explains the IAP. If Johnny is to be assessed for special education, you give your signed consent, an assessment is done, and then a new team takes over. This team, the IEP (Individual Education Plan) team, has a minimum of three members: a school administrator (or designee), the classroom teacher, and you, the parent. The team writes its IEP, which is a document giving assessment results and a plan of exactly how Johnny's needs will be met.

How Bad Must Johnny's Problems Be to Constitute a Learning Disability?

Each state has its own eligibility guidelines for SLD, but as a rough rule, Johnny has to be about 2 years below the expected level of performance for his age to qualify.

What *Is* Special Education?

If Johnny qualifies as having SLD, he gets special education services. Special education today is not so much categories of provision as a response to individual need. It is the range of services (big or small) deemed necessary for Johnny by his IEP team. If Johnny qualifies for special education, he must, by law, be provided with the "least restrictive environment" for him personally, whatever that may be. Some examples of special education you see in schools are:

- Students are taught their own programs in separate classes.
- A resource specialist (who used to be called a remedial teacher) takes individuals or small groups from regular class to go for lessons with her. (She can see Johnny any number of times each week.)
- A resource specialist comes into a regular class to help individuals or small groups with their regular work.
- A resource specialist advises the classroom teacher and helps modify work.

Reading Problems—The Facts

- About 17 percent of America's children (10 million) struggle to read.
- In reading tests, boys score lower than girls and are identified as having learning problems far more often than girls.
- One in three children is a year or more behind in school.
- About half the young adults with a criminal history have reading problems.

Could Johnny Be Dyslexic?

Dyslexia is a subset of SLD. In simple terms, a child is dyslexic if he is of average (or above) intelligence but is unexpectedly and enduringly unable to read. Johnny may fit this description, and may even be called dyslexic by a private tester, but this won't count in school. Johnny won't be officially considered dyslexic, or get special education services, unless he has qualified under school district tests or tests the district has approved.

Dyslexia as Defined by the Learning Disabilities Association of America

Dyslexia is a learning disability in the area of reading. It is included in the category of "Learning Disabilities" in the Individuals with Disabilities Education Act (IDEA). A person with dyslexia is someone with average to above average intelligence whose problem in reading is not the result of emotional problems, lack of motivation, poor teaching, mental retardation, or vision or hearing deficits. The term *dyslexia*, however, is defined in different ways. While reading is the basic problem, people include different aspects of reading and related problems in their definitions.

Dyslexia Facts

- Genetic factors account for about half of someone's risk of developing dyslexia, although no single gene is likely to be to blame.
- Dyslexics have brain differences that show up on brain scans.
- Diagnosing a learning disability is notoriously subjective. Even though we know there are neurological and genetic factors, social and educational factors impact too.

CHILDREN WHO STRUGGLE WITH READING BUT DON'T HAVE DISABILITIES

This is a huge group, and your son's probably in it. Many thousands of children who can't read and look as if they should surely get extra help, don't. They don't meet the eligibility requirements for special education. If Johnny doesn't qualify for special education, he gets whatever help your school chooses to provide, in accordance with Section 504 of the Rehabilitation Act.* This requires schools to make "reasonable accommodations" for struggling learners, but "reasonable accommodations" can translate into anything. Find out exactly what your school will do. Some schools provide regular help with a teacher when they can or run programs. Programs typically happen periodically and for a limited time. If Johnny's school has many children from low-income families, it may operate the "Title I" program, which gives special tutorial help to underachieving children.

IF JOHNNY DOESN'T QUALIFY FOR SPECIAL EDUCATION

If Johnny doesn't qualify for special education, your options are to:

- Have Johnny included in existing programs at school (reading, tutoring, homework)
- Ask his teacher to help you be his tutor at home

---

*Section 504 of the Rehabilitation Act (1973) mandates that schools make reasonable accommodations for struggling learners (those who don't qualify as learning-disabled) and have a Section 504 official. If you get into a battle, ask for the district "Parents' Rights Manual," see the Section 504 official, and/or go to your district (the superintendent is the highest-level person). Contact the Learning Disabilities Association of America (some members have fought their own child's case).

- Start a tutoring program at school yourself
- Get outside tutoring
- Change schools
- Home school

IN SHORT

- "Specific Learning Disabilities" (SLD) is one of the 13 federal categories of disability, and dyslexia is a subset of SLD.
- Though you will hear these terms used widely, they are not recognized by your school district, and Johnny won't get special education services, unless he qualifies under district or district-approved tests.
- Whatever Johnny's difficulties, he needs to get practical help quickly.

2

The Second Way: Get More Help at School

Good schools run programs to help struggling readers. It's important to ask for help in an assertive, specific, but nonconfrontational way.

CHAPTER 3

How Do I Recognize a Good School?

A GOOD SCHOOL MEETS JOHNNY'S NEEDS

Boy's Need	How a School Might Make Provision
Movement and activity	A good school will allow movement in class and provide hands-on experiences.
Friends the same age	If you have delayed school for a year, you may want Johnny to start school with other boys who have done the same.
Lack of distraction	Some parents like single-sex schools. They feel that in boy-only reading classes, boys can't feel embarrassed by the presence or superior performance of girls.
Social skills	Social skills are particularly important for a boy with reading problems, so a mixed-sex school may be best. Johnny can learn how to recruit help and be liked by all people. In later life, it's usually personable people who have jobs and friends.

Boy's Need	How a School Might Make Provision
A smaller, more personal school	Johnny may do better in a school where he sees fewer teachers and makes better social ties.
Smaller classes	Theoretically, a teacher with fewer children in the class has more time for each one. Ask about the number of children in Johnny's class. Private schools may not guarantee smaller classes.
Male teachers	Single moms in particular may see this as very important.
Good instruction	The single most important influence will be the classroom teacher.
Special programs	Special tutoring and reading programs give small-group instruction. Struggling readers need this extra help.
Help with homework	Homework clubs are usually run by a teacher, who may get older kids to help too. Kids like homework clubs. They get help, and they get to hang out with friends too. Parents like them because homework is done right after school, leaving evenings less busy. If Johnny goes to a homework club, there's a good chance his attitude and grades will improve.

School Programs

At the start of this book, I said that Johnny's classroom teacher is the most important influence on his success in school. What comes second?

Of all the things to look at in a school, take careful note of the special programs it offers. Schools voluntarily help kids who struggle but don't receive special education services, but the extent of this help varies from school to school. A school that offers tutoring with volunteer parents, time with a reading teacher, and a homework club, is better for Johnny than a school whose programs are geared mostly toward the high achievers.

Reading or Tutoring Programs

Since these programs are nearly always for small groups, Johnny will get more attention here. If the program is offered by volunteers or peers, the option is still a good one.

School programs can be run by:

- Classroom teachers who teach whole classes
- Teachers who teach small groups or individuals
- Volunteers or peers who teach small groups or individuals

Programs Run by Classroom Teachers for the Whole Class

Watch that you don't get misled by these "programs," thinking they're the type for small groups. When teachers talk of literacy programs or literacy initiatives, check out exactly who the program is for. When a teacher says a program is good for poor readers, she may simply be telling you how good the classroom program is. She's telling you Johnny is getting, or will get, the same instruction as all the other children in class.

Personal/Social Development Programs

These programs aren't reading programs, of course, but they're well worth looking out for. Teachers (often outgoing, well-liked ones) run classes to teach Johnny cooperative behavior. He gets to play games and do fun, group activities. This is great for developing his social skills.

Programs Run by Teachers for Small Groups or Individuals

These programs may be fairly informal, with a teacher taking on the job of being the reading teacher, or more formal, with a teacher who is specially trained to teach a particular reading program (Reading Recovery, Orton-Gillingham, Slingerland, LIPS, Lindamood-Bell).

Competition for places in reading programs is usually fierce. Be sure to promote Johnny's case. If you're comparing programs in different schools, ask how many hours per week Johnny would be in a reading program. Advertising makes all programs seem wonderful, but in reality some may only give Johnny a short time each week.

Real Life: Michael Gets Help from School

Even when Michael was a baby, Beth read to him. In his preschool years, she read or drew with him most days, and when he was 5, he started school with confidence and optimism.

In grade 1, Michael hadn't started to read. Most children in his class were reading simple books, and many were taking chapter books home. Michael only knew a handful of words and didn't like reading and writing. It took him ages to write simple sentences, and he was often left at the table long after the other kids had completed their writing. Beth was concerned. Her brother was dyslexic. She asked the teacher if Michael needed extra tutoring. The teacher assured her it was early days and there was nothing to worry about. Michael had plenty of time to catch up, a delay was not unusual in children his age. Michael finished grade 1 happily.

In grade 2, Beth again asked about Michael's progress. Did he have learning disabilities? No, he didn't, she was told, and there was no need for assessment because he certainly wouldn't qualify for special education. Beth proposed private tutoring to Michael. "No," said Michael, now 7. "You can't force me to go."

Grade 3 came around, and Michael turned 8. He could only read beginners' books, and Beth felt something had to change. She decided to have Michael tutored, regardless of his complaints, and she wanted practical help at school, too. She enrolled Michael at a learning center, where he went twice each week, and made his soccer practices and play dates contingent on his attendance at the center. At school Michael was put in a small group of four children who saw the reading teacher for 40 minutes every day.

Michael is now in grade 5. He went to the learning center for 6 months and stayed with the reading teacher all through grade 3. In grade 4, he saw the reading teacher twice each week, and still does. Beth feels he made the best progress when he was having daily lessons with the reading teacher. She thinks having special lessons twice a week is great, but having them every day was best of all.

These days Michael gets A's on his school reports, and Beth is confident he'll cope fine with middle school next year.

When Johnny Moves Up a Grade

When Johnny moves up a grade, be sure to tell his new teacher about the programs he's been in so she'll think about putting him in a program again. Sometimes this information isn't passed between teachers, so it's up to us to check.

PROGRAMS RUN BY VOLUNTEERS OR PEERS IN SCHOOL

Reading

In some schools, volunteers, often parents, run reading or tutoring programs. Volunteers are usually conscientious people who can help Johnny gain confidence and progress with reading.

Real Life: Colette Starts a Tutoring Club

Every week Colette helped in her daughter's fourth-grade class. The children had to complete several reports, and Colette helped them prepare and organize their notes. She tried to spend the most time with three boys who clearly weren't keeping up. Other kids brought neat piles of notes to class, with long tables of contents and elaborate illustrations. The three boys had a few crumpled sheets of muddled sentences.

Colette couldn't stop thinking about the three struggling boys. She stayed behind after class one day and spoke to the teacher, Mrs. White. The idea of a tutoring club was born.

The first step Colette took after talking to Mrs. White was to put her idea to the PTA. Meanwhile, Mrs. White went to the school principal. Everyone was enthusiastic, so Colette contacted a nearby school whose tutoring program had established a great reputation. She was invited to a training session.

By word of mouth, Colette recruited 16 parents for her new tutoring program. She didn't need to advertise. The only "cold call" she made was to a man she thought would be "just great" at tutoring. She had it in mind to pair him with one boy who didn't live with his father and seemed to be crying out for a good male mentor. The man became the one highly valuable male tutor.

The volunteer tutors committed themselves to two or three weekly sessions with one child, 30 minutes each session. Teachers chose children from the fourth and fifth grades who didn't qualify for special education, but were nevertheless unable to keep up in class, giving preference to the fifth graders (who were approaching high school). A letter was sent to parents, and every parent consented to the tutoring. The PTA donated $500 for resources, with a further $750 per semester (this was a strong PTA!). The resources were housed in the reading teacher's room, the principal said sessions could run during school hours, and the tutoring began.

What worked? What was hard? In Colette's words, "Everyone was enthusiastic, and that made it work. The teachers knew we could do things that would make a difference. As Mrs. White said, 'These kids will feel honored to have you there just for them. You'll teach them a lot, and you'll do wonders for their self esteem, too.'" What was hard? "Well, kids have good and bad days, and the bad days were hard. But when my student told me he didn't want to do his report and didn't want to see me again, I told him straight back I wasn't leaving and we had to do the report. The end result of my hanging in there was he handed in every report. He'd never done that before. I felt I'd really changed a kid's life, and I know everyone felt that way. We all felt the tutoring was the best thing we'd ever done at school. Over the weeks you really saw the progress; it was absolutely worthwhile. All 16 tutors want to continue tutoring next year, and I've been phoned by three other schools too."

Do you have any tips for prospective tutors?

- "Have one parent organizer and one teacher representative. This helps communication between everyone.
- "Tutors met three times per semester. We all enjoyed the meetings, and felt a sense of camaraderie. At one meeting a reading specialist gave a presentation.
- "We didn't use a reward scheme, and that was good. Mrs. White thought the kids would feel so special that tangible rewards wouldn't be needed. She was right, and one advantage was that no child got more or less than the others.
- "The school that advised us has 25 kids in its program and 18 tutors. Some of the tutors have two kids to work with. We don't do that, and I'm not sure I'd be able to have two kids. It's very intense and personal, and I feel one child is best.

- "Our program evolved. At first we did basic skills, but then we worked on reports and homework. The kids wanted to do real work that would be graded by the teacher. We were able to do it because the teachers were always happy to talk to us after class."

The final word? "The grade 5 kids were basically on their last chance. We truly felt we might be saving them from behavior problems in high school. It was so important. So vital. I'd recommend it to anyone."

Peer Tutoring/Buddying/Mentoring

An assured way to get a boy to do a thing is to have him see an admired older boy do it. Schools use peer tutoring programs and buddy systems to capitalize on this. Great results can happen when kids help other kids, so if your school operates a program, try to have Johnny included. If your school doesn't run such programs, suggest they do!

What Do Reading Programs Teach?

Reading programs teach:

Sight words (words that must be automatically identified)

Phonics and phonemic awareness (sounding out)

Reading

Grammar (constructing sentences properly)

Comprehension (understanding)

All reading programs teach these things, but the way they teach them will differ. Ask how much time Johnny will get on the program, who'll be teaching him, and whether he'll be taught in a group or by himself. Private reading centers in particular all have their own methods and distinct ways of motivating children.

Phonemic Awareness

Teaching phonemic awareness is teaching about sounds. Having kids listen to sounds and make sound groups (like *pat, hat, mat*) is called *phonemic awareness*. This teaching comes before teaching letters and continues as a big part of any phonics instruction.

IN SHORT

- Good schools have reading or tutoring programs; they may be run by teachers, volunteers, or peers. Ask to have Johnny included in these programs and let his teacher know what difficulties he has and what help he's had before.

CHAPTER 4

Parent-Teacher Conferences

HOW THINGS USED TO BE

Years ago, my parents went to "Parents' Evening" to discuss my progress. The teacher said things like, "She should try harder," and my report included comments like:

"Tracey talks too much."
"Tracey thinks she's the teacher."

My mother read school reports with complete agreement (and some amusement). If boys in my class got "the slipper" whacked across their backsides by a teacher, no outraged parent sued. Teachers were treated as authorities, and children were told the teacher was right, usually no matter what.

TODAY'S SCHOOL REPORTS

It's different now, and rightly so. We expect our children to be treated with dignity and respect, and we're prepared to challenge teachers who we think lack good judgment. We want the teacher to guide Johnny's behavior without diminishing him in any way, and if Johnny has problems, we expect the teacher to modify the learning environment to accommodate his needs. This is reasonable by today's standards. But with these new standards comes a new style of reports, much more formal and carefully worded. Today we read computer-generated comments phrased to describe only what Johnny has demonstrated. They tell us things like, Johnny:

- Demonstrates an interest in reading
- Uses appropriate word analysis
- Applies strategies when reading (e.g., prediction, context clues, self-monitoring)

For each "criterion," Johnny's score is a letter like:

H (Producing high-quality work consistently)
S (Progressing satisfactorily)
N (Improvement needed)
N/A (Not applicable)

Interestingly, these reports can misrepresent Johnny because of their design. When the teacher gives scores for each term on the same report, so you can see Johnny's progress through the year, she might purposely start with low scores to allow for improvement. Then you might see something like:

"Meets the standard"

when you expected:

"Exceeds the standard"

As one teacher put it,

"If I give him the top mark now, I'll have nowhere to go."

COMMENTS FROM THE TEACHER

Most of us dislike reading through the dreary criteria and working out what the S or H stands for. We go quickly to the teacher's comments, and want to know the basics:

He really dislikes reading, and just can't do it. It's all so hard for him that he doesn't want to try. It's humiliating for him. He hasn't made progress with reading, and seems to be where he was in grade 1. Have you noticed he's unhappy? Can you explain to me what the school does for children who are falling steadily behind like this?"

Notice that you haven't blamed the teacher. You've simply stated what you see and asked for more information. You haven't begun a confrontation with Johnny's teacher.

You might continue the conversation by offering to do different homework with Johnny. You could say you'd be willing to work through any remedial books with him. If you aren't good at talking with teachers, and feel you need help, see if you can find an advocate. Maybe you have a friend who's good at talking to professionals. This person should either meet with teachers on your behalf and report back to you or go with you to meetings.

If Johnny's problems aren't helped by the classroom teacher, see someone else in school—the vice principal, principal, school psychologist, school district psychologist, or school counselor. Join the school PTA to lobby for your concerns and go to the district education office. Groups for parents of children with reading difficulties can give you advice and support, too.

WHAT NOW?

You've given Johnny's teacher information about Johnny's problems, now it's time to focus on solutions. What practical help can we give? Here are a few simple strategies that have helped other boys:

Strategy	What to Watch Out For
Putting Johnny in tutoring or homework programs	You should regularly ask Johnny how he's doing and look at his work to be sure he's keeping up.
Giving Johnny large print and simpler text	You must decide who simplifies the text—the teacher, the teacher's helper, another student, you?
Moving Johnny to the front of the class so he can see and hear better	First be sure Johnny won't feel the teacher is picking on him.
Giving Johnny a buddy	Buddies must be carefully chosen and perhaps changed after a few weeks. You must state clearly what the buddy's job is (checking Johnny has his homework packed; writing answers Johnny dictates; reading with Johnny) and train him.
Having Johnny do less and/or different homework	Make sure Johnny likes the way homework is changed. If he hates typing, it's no good suggesting he use a computer unless you first find a fun learn-to-type program and have him do it as homework until he's competent.
You tutor Johnny in school	Teachers often have simple kits a parent can teach from. The SRA kits are especially user-friendly, but first the teacher must think this is a good idea and organize it into the schedule.
You tutor Johnny at home	It's best to have a helpful teacher who is willing to give you some pointers.
Johnny gets private tutoring with support from school	A teacher can give Johnny less homework so he can do work for a reading specialist, but first she must think this is a great idea.

> ### *Embarrassment May Always Be an Issue for Johnny*
> Johnny may be embarrassed because he notices he's different and feels it, even if he pretends not to. It's up to us to explain to Johnny as best we can, and as often as he needs, that he's not "dumb."

What Makes Practical Strategies Work?

Incentives and support help Johnny succeed. Whatever practical solutions we plan, we should make sure Johnny is able to succeed. If we nag or punish him for what we see as his laziness or defiance, he'll learn to hate our involvement (and may feel generally hateful too).

Real Life: Lazy Greg

I have an adult friend, Greg, who was "remedial" in school. He describes his school days as terrible, a time when he learned nothing. What went so wrong for Greg? In short, people thought he was lazy and trying to "get away with it."

Greg's parents sent him for private tutoring after school. He hated every lesson. He was never ready to go, complained bitterly, and more often than not had to be physically dragged to the car. His parents, worn out and at the end of their patience, said he was ungrateful and, of course, lazy.

Reading problems can cause mayhem in a family, largely because parents feel guilty and worried. They fear a jobless, hopeless future for their child. Usually they have no one to help and advise them. Stress is high, nerves are stretched, anxiety brings harsh words.

Today Greg owns a cleaning business and has several employees. He can't read, but tells his clients he's dyslexic and gets help with written work. When I ask him about his reading problems, Greg says he rarely notices (except for the time he came to watch a video with me, and I selected a foreign subtitled movie!). He manages, and may one day try again with the reading. He's a favorite with all the children in his own family and is especially good at seeing through a child's grumbles. "Of course a kid acts tough or disinterested," says Greg. "What else can he do to keep his dignity?"

Real Life: The Peace-Keeping Principal

In his first week at a new school, 8-year-old Lenny didn't complete his writing and was kept in class at recess. His mom, Kim, met the teacher:

> "Lenny really enjoys your class and is happy here. I'm concerned, though, when he tells me he's kept in at recess for not completing his writing. Could you tell me about this, please?"

The teacher said Lenny had been kept in to teach him the consequences of being disorganized. If he applied himself better, he would complete his work. Kim replied that keeping Lenny in at recess was creating new problems. He didn't get to socialize, so his new school wasn't fun for him, and he was starting to hate writing, too. Kim asked if Lenny could sit away from the others to complete his work in class, if distractibility was the problem, or if he could finish his work at home.

The teacher was adamant that she couldn't make a special case for Lenny, so Kim ended the meeting (it really wasn't going anywhere) with a potential follow-up. She asked that if Lenny was kept in over the next 2 weeks, she be sent a letter each time, so another meeting could be planned. A few days later, Lenny came home in tears. He had handed in a report, and the teacher had handed it back, saying it wasn't long enough. Kim went to the principal.

The principal suggested an incentive scheme for Lenny. He would get stickers for completing his writing and a reward from Kim at the end of a week if he had received stickers each day. The rejected report would be accepted with one extra sheet of writing, which Lenny would dictate for Kim to type (so it wouldn't be arduous).

For the next few weeks, the rewards system helped Lenny, and for the rest of that year he wasn't kept in during recess. The principal's focus on positive, practical solutions broke through what had seemed like an impasse. Kim was relieved and very thankful, and she adopted some practical solutions of her own. She helped Lenny with future reports and homework instead of leaving him to work alone (because, despite the bad start, the teacher was right about Lenny being disorganized!).

FINISH THE MEETING BY SCHEDULING A FOLLOW-UP

End a first parent-teacher conference with something like:

> "I'd like to arrange a meeting in 3 weeks' time to review progress."

Or maybe ask that a note to be sent to you at the end of each week. Arrange a meeting with the reading teacher or the principal. Arrange something. Then the teacher will know you're not going away and won't forget your concerns.

IN SHORT

- List for yourself the few pieces of information you'll give the teacher.
- Phrase your points in terms of your son's distress, not the teacher's shortcomings.
- List for yourself practical strategies that could help.
- Plan a follow-up.

PART 3

The Third Way: Find an Excellent Tutor or Be One Yourself

Struggling children need extra help. The best help is frequent, personal instruction. The instruction can be given in school by a teacher, another student, or a volunteer; it can be given by an outside tutor; or it can be given by a mixture of these people. If you do the job yourself, you should follow the same type of plan that the experts use.

CHAPTER 5

Do I Need to Get Outside Help?

REASONS TO GET OUTSIDE HELP

- You and/or Johnny are worried.
- Johnny gets help at school, but it makes no difference.
- Johnny won't go into school programs (he doesn't want to be teased by other kids).
- You feel too close to the problem to give help yourself.

Worry Is a Good Reason to Get Help

A parent's instincts are usually right. If you're worried, chances are Johnny isn't doing his best at school and tutoring will help. If Johnny's worried, tutoring will move him away from worry and into action. Match Johnny with a tutor or center he likes, build a routine, and stick with it. Studies show tutoring helps, and frequent, consistent help is best. Monitor Johnny's performance and attitude, and make changes if you need to. Does the time suit him? (Maybe he misses sports and hates that.) Is the work at just the right level? (Not too easy or too hard.) Is he getting enough success? (Do we consciously give recognition?)

Johnny Gets Help at School, but It Makes No Difference

Struggling readers need regular help at their own personal level of performance. This kind of help may simply be more than

Johnny's school, within the limits of its budget and available staff, can give. An outside tutor, whose job it is to provide individualized instruction, can plan a program in which Johnny works specifically on his weak skills every night.

Johnny Won't Go into School Programs

This problem affects older boys in particular. At about age 10, Johnny becomes concerned with image and acceptance and will carefully cultivate the prevailing cool image. He won't want to be different from his friends, so he may refuse extra help in school. Sometimes it's not worth a battle, especially if you've heard of a good tutor.

Here are a few things to consider with older boys and tutoring:

Typical Traits	What Helps
Johnny is obsessed with rules. He wants to know who's in charge and what the rules are, and heaven help any hapless rule breaker!	A clear schedule and firm rules will impress Johnny now. He may consider anyone lacking management and organizational skills to be pretty worthless.
He's more private. He probably doesn't want you to ask about schoolwork or help him with reading.	A tutor has emotional distance, and Johnny knows she works with boys like him all the time. The tutor won't secretly judge him and probably knows what she's doing (unlike mom, of course!).
Johnny's efforts to distance himself from you make him especially vulnerable.	Extended family, close friends, church and social groups are invaluable now. If you don't have a support network, it's worth encouraging Johnny to play sports and join clubs. Hopefully he'll gravitate toward trustworthy friends and mentors.

Typical Traits	What Helps
Johnny starts to think about life beyond the classroom and knows that jobs require at least some literacy.	Johnny may now be nervous about his prospects and more willing to be tutored or to attend extra classes.
Johnny is infuriatingly arrogant.	Hang in there! When he's condescending toward teachers and tutors, let it roll off you. For reasons we can't fathom, it seems he just needs to be this way for now!
It's important that instruction isn't "babyish."	Books and worksheets must be of high interest with low-level vocabulary. Johnny wants mature themes, but he still needs simple text. It's hard to find books like this, but good teachers and librarians can help.

You Feel Too Close to the Problem to Give Help

Very often the best help a parent can give is to let someone else deal with the problem. Parents have all the emotional involvement. We get upset, and want so much for Johnny to succeed that our vision is clouded. If we delegate the job to someone trained, we can feel relief and put our efforts into building Johnny's confidence. We can be the person who nurtures rather than forces, helps rather than hinders. Johnny can never get enough support and encouragement, and wants it most of all from mom and dad.

Real Life: Monica, a Teacher, Doesn't Tutor Her Own Children

Monica taught one of my children in elementary school. She was wonderful. When I watched how Monica treated my child, I wanted to copy everything she did. I wanted to store up everything I saw, then rush home and write it down, so I too could be as nice to my own child. I wanted to talk like her, prepare activities like her, and generally be her.

Monica had three children of her own. One day, when I was talking to her about the work I was doing, she told me that two of her children had been tutored. I was amazed. I had thought I was the only teacher who was guilty of not wanting to teach my own children. But here was Monica, perfect Monica, openly and cheerfully telling me about having had tutors for her children.

"Oh, no, I wouldn't dream of teaching my own kids," said a smiling Monica.

"I have this lovely teacher friend who stopped work to have a baby and in that time did some tutoring at home. I was so lucky to get her, and my son progressed beautifully. I know if I had tutored my own kids, I would've been awful. I sent my other son to a learning center, and he liked it because he had young teachers and got to shoot balls in a basketball net. That center was a cool place for boys. I could never have got my son to agree to being taught by me, even if I'd been crazy enough to consider it!"

Monica was, after all, a typical mom, very glad to get help.

Who Gives Help?

People who help children with reading call themselves all sorts of names: practitioner, therapist, counselor, teacher, tutor, and consultant are just some of them. Ask about qualifications and membership in professional organizations. Consultants and therapists are usually more qualified and more expensive.

WHO WILL BE A GOOD TUTOR?

After cost, our choice of tutor or learning center will mostly depend on Johnny's personality. Does he like a formal or an informal classroom, computers or personal attention, working with a group or working alone? For general guidelines, consider the following:

- Lessons should be structured and sequential so Johnny learns one step at a time.
- He should master a skill before moving to the next.
- He should understand why he's learning a skill.
- He should be encouraged and rewarded.
- He should like, or at least not mind, the tutoring.
- You should be shown test results and/or examples of Johnny's work that chart his progress.
- You should get regular and simply stated feedback.

If all these factors are being addressed, you can be fairly sure you're getting good instruction.

The Cost of Tutoring

Prices charged for tutoring start at about $35 an hour. Individual tutoring is more expensive than small-group instruction. To find volunteer tutors outside of school, ask at your local council or library.

Real Life: Jenny Finds Great Help

Sam, age 8, couldn't read well. In particular, he hated doing homework. Everything would start off fairly well, but when Sam found sentence after sentence he couldn't read, he would fly into a rage. Jenny knew she should defuse the situation, but, like Sam, she couldn't sustain her best efforts. She'd begin with encouraging words like:

"It's not really so hard, let's try again."

But when Sam continued to rage, she'd end up joining him. Without meaning to, she usually criticized, too, saying things like:

"You never stick at it."

"You have to get more self-control."

Sam's teacher told Jenny that Sam certainly didn't qualify for special education. He was being given some help when the school could spare a teacher to work with him, but that didn't happen often. Sam made no progress, and the homework fights continued.

Jenny decided to try private tutoring. At first she employed a college student who worked with Sam once a week for 8 weeks. Sam liked the student and did the work she set. His mom was pleased, but had a nagging suspicion the work wasn't quite focused enough. It seemed to lack planning and direction. She took Sam to a learning center. Before he went, he complained bitterly. How could she stop him seeing the young student, who was a perfectly good tutor? He didn't want to see a bunch of dreary old teachers. It was geeky. What if someone saw him? When he got there, he was subdued by the authoritative air of the place, and listened obligingly with his mother. She breathed a sigh of relief.

Jenny stayed in an adjoining room while Sam did his first introductory lesson. She tried to read, but couldn't help wondering if she had done the right thing. Sam had been happy with his young student tutor. What if he now refused to come to this center?

By the time Sam finished his lesson, Jenny was a nervous wreck. Would Sam be stubborn, or could she enroll him at this center? Jenny quizzed the subdued Sam. It seemed he'd had his show of defiance, but could see the sense in coming to the new center. Sure it was different from what he was used to, but he'd come to it!

Sam attended the center until the end of elementary school. He was tutored by a qualified teacher who knew about motivating children. He made good progress, and felt confident and well prepared when he started middle school. Jenny said the tutoring changed both their lives.

Real Life: David Responds to Tightly Structured Tutoring

When I first met 10-year-old David, he could only read two- and three-letter words. His mom said he had received every type of help from school, but nothing had been any use. She was distraught because David still couldn't read, and blamed his teachers:

> "One kept sending home flash cards that were useless. David had no idea what the cards were for and didn't want to use them. In fact, I said I didn't think the cards were helping, but the teacher kept sending them home. Then she left and another teacher came. That teacher did different things, but she left to have a baby. After that he didn't see any teachers, just a mom who volunteered as a tutor but only showed up now and then."

I started tutoring David, and began by telling his mom about the SPRint way of catching up (see Chapter 6). I told David and his mom what homework David would be doing, and assured them he would always be shown why and how a task should be done before being left to do it unassisted. I explained the routine we would follow, and we made a schedule. I told David and his mom that if they made homework a solid routine, they would see results.

David and his mom both worked hard, he with doing assignments, she with supporting. Whenever David grew weary, his mom would cajole and encourage, and soon he began to take pride in his achievements. His teacher, seeing his progress, agreed to stop setting homework so he could instead do the homework

I set. His mom was delighted; she no longer had to battle with school homework or dry David's tears and listen to his heart-wrenching complaints. Her main hope was for David to start high school able to read basic text. She worried that in high school David might cut class if he couldn't read, and, like all moms, she worried about drugs and bad company. She knew school difficulties might send David down wrong paths.

David started high school having been tutored three times a week for a whole school year. He could read basic text and was optimistic. He was accepted into a reading program in the new high school, so his continued progress looked assured. David never cut class, and to the best of my knowledge, he didn't get into any of the trouble his mom had feared. A program of frequent, regular, and structured instruction had moved David forward when he thought he was stuck for good.

IN SHORT

- Choose an individual or center that suits Johnny's personality and will chart his progress in simple terms.
- Have a steady tutoring routine; 10 to 40 minutes daily gives great results.
- If Johnny is asked to do homework for a private tutor, ask his classroom teacher to help. Can she give less homework so Johnny can work on the tutor's homework? Teachers can be helpful if they know the tutor uses a structured program that meets Johnny's specific needs.

CHAPTER 6

Tutoring Johnny Yourself: What to Teach

THE THREE ESSENTIALS

To teach reading systematically and well, teach the SPRint way:

1. **S**ight words
2. **P**honics
3. **R**eading

How Often?

Have one or two 1-hour lessons every week and 10 to 40 minutes homework daily. You will see Johnny surge forward after just a few weeks. At the end of 12 weeks, Johnny will be at a new level of reading.

Learning Facts

- Positives, incentives, and rewards improve learning.
- Imposed negative consequences or punishments can teach a boy to suppress anger and vengeful feelings or hide misbehavior in future.
- We are able to retrieve only five to nine items from short-term memory.

- Long-term memory relies on meaning. In order to recall a lot of stored information, our memory has to be jogged by a small piece of readily available information. This is demonstrated by the use of mnemonics (ways to jog our memory). We can recall large pieces of information by first recalling songs or rhymes that remind us of the information. Hence "Every good boy deserves fruit," "30 days has September," and so on.
- Boys who have to work hard on reading may seem highly distractible.
- When we feel we own our work and don't have to suffer interference, we work more willingly and enthusiastically.

What We Should Do

Make sure we reward, encourage, and nurture our boys and expect their teachers to do the same.

Focus on solutions. When punishments are unavoidable, make them immediate and more symbolic than concrete. In other words, make much of the fact that you are disappointed and make the punishment seem serious. Punishments can then be kept within limits. Avoid giving out harsh punishments in anger. Punishments like being grounded for 2 months may seem OK in the heat of the moment, but won't achieve any more than an "I'm disappointed" talk and grounding for 1 week. "Time-outs" should be time apart to calm down, with access to books or quiet activities.

Rote learning* of many facts should be avoided. Break tasks into small parts, and look for rhymes, acronyms, and other memory aids.

---

*Rote learning is memorizing through repetition without giving any attention to principles or meanings. We usually learn the times tables by rote learning, but when children attach tunes or rhymes, the learning is easier and longer-lasting. Tunes, rhymes, and meanings are memory aids (mnemonics).

Ask Johnny what kind of environment helps him work. Most kids these days like low-level background noise and hate our old-fashioned notion of quiet!

Always adopt a hands-off approach when you offer help. Don't hold Johnny's book or paper unless he offers it or you have asked permission. Such subtleties make a difference. Be a genuine support rather than an interference. Say things like:

"Would you like help?"

"Would you like me to look at it?"

"If you need any help, just call. I'll be right here."

The SPRint Lesson

How	What	Example 1-Hour Lesson
• Fun and positives	• Sight words	1. **Sight words** (15 minutes)
• Routine and repetition	• Phonics	Using the word folder,
• One-step-at-a-time, hands-off instruction	• Reading	• Test the last lesson's 10 words.*
		• Give 10 new sight words and practice them in games.
		Break: 5 minutes
		2. **Phonics** (20 minutes)
		Use sheets, books, letter cards, or flash cards to teach phonics and spelling. Do a short dictation, too.
		Break: 10 minutes

*We use 10 words even though short-term memory stores 5 to 9 items because Johnny won't need to rely on recall alone, as many words or word parts can be sounded out.

How	What	Example 1-Hour Lesson
		3. **Reading** (5 minutes)
		Look at this week's new reading book. Practice unknown words, discuss the cover and illustrations, and read it together if that's what Johnny wants.
		4. **Give homework** (5 minutes)
		Homework will always include
		• Moving words up in the word folder from pocket 1 to pocket 6.
		• Phonics activities (a page from a workbook; 20 flash cards; a game of phonics bingo)
		• Reading a book (with or without assistance)

PART 1 OF A SPRINT LESSON

Sight Words

Divide your hour into three parts. In the first part, deal with sight words. Sight words are the words that make up about 70 percent of what we read. They are also called "most common words" or "high-frequency words," and we learn them to a level of automatic recognition because they occur so frequently in text. We want Johnny to work through a list of sight words a few at a time, until he knows all of these words by sight.

Sight Words Are Not "Look and Say" Words

Many people rightly object to children learning hundreds of words by their appearance. These sight words aren't like that at all. We call them sight words because we learn them to a level of automatic recognition, or by sight, but to achieve that, we sound them out whenever we can and learn word families (discussed later in this chapter) to help us remember common letter groupings.

Why We Must Know Sight Words by Sight

When Johnny instantly identifies the frequently occurring words, his reading fluency increases dramatically. He's 70 percent closer to good reading (remember sight words account for 70 percent of all words), and because he reads more fluently, he has better comprehension, which in turn helps him figure out hard words.

List of 220 Sight Words

a	any	been	but	could	eat
about	are	before	buy	cut	eight
after	around	best	by	did	every
again	as	better	call	do	fall
all	ask	big	came	does	far
as	at	black	can	done	fast
always	ate	blue	carry	don't	find
am	away	both	clean	down	first
an	be	bring	cold	draw	five
and	because	brown	come	drink	fly

for	how	much	put	tell	walk
found	hurt	must	ran	ten	want
four	I	my	read	thank	warm
from	if	myself	red	that	was
full	in	never	ride	the	wash
funny	into	new	right	their	we
gave	is	no	round	them	well
get	it	not	run	then	went
give	its	now	said	there	were
go	jump	of	saw	these	what
goes	just	off	say	they	when
going	keep	old	see	think	where
good	kind	on	seven	this	which
got	know	once	shall	those	white
green	laugh	one	she	three	who
grow	let	only	show	to	why
had	light	open	sing	today	will
has	like	or	sit	together	wish
have	little	our	six	too	with
he	live	out	sleep	try	work
help	long	over	small	two	would
her	look	own	so	under	write
here	made	pick	some	up	yellow
him	make	play	soon	upon	yes
his	many	please	start	us	you
hold	may	pretty	stop	use	your
hot	me	pull	take	very	

You'll Find Sight Word Lists on Many Web Sites

This list, called the Dolch Sight Vocabulary, is available at www.readingpains.com.

How to Teach Sight Words

The word folder is a fun and effective way to teach sight words. Words go into pocket 1 of the folder, then Johnny gets tested—he reads out the words or writes them down for you to see. Correct words go up to pocket 2. Later Johnny gets tested again and correct words move up to pocket 3, and so on. Use the word folder for the first part of every lesson and for homework.

Using All 200 Words

Many teachers work with only the first 100 sight words, but using the entire 220 will be worth the effort in the long run.

The Word Folder

Making the Word Folder

Get a manila folder. Johnny chooses, carries, decorates (with anything he likes), and generally takes full possession of it. On the

front cover, Johnny writes "Words" (or you write it if he wants you to). On the inside right page, stick six pockets. Make the pockets from rectangles of card taped down on three sides or buy library card pockets at a school supplies store. Arrange and number the pockets, and put one big pocket labeled "Done" on the inside left page.

Choosing Words

Each lesson, put 10 words in the word folder. To get 10 words, have Johnny read through the list of 220 sight words until you have 10 words he doesn't know. If he already knows a word, skip that one. Write each new word on a card or ticket (cut up your own pieces of paper), and put all 10 into pocket 1 after you've studied them (for word families, sounding out, and words inside words) and played games with them.

Also Use Your Folder for Any Hard Words You Come Across in Reading Books

Often you'll read an easy book and find hard words in it. You might read, "The cats were on the mat," and Johnny doesn't know *were*. Write *were* on a card and put it in the word folder. Explain that this word isn't easy to sound out, so we remember it mostly by sight.

Try to Sound Out Words and Make Word Families

Before putting a new word in the word folder, ask:

- Can parts of the word be sounded out?
- Does the word belong to a word family?
- Are there any smaller words inside the word?

Sounding out, making word families, and finding words inside words all help Johnny memorize.

Word Families

Word families are groups of words that rhyme and have the same spelling pattern. Words like *small, call, fall, ball, tall,* and *wall* belong to the *-all* family. If you come upon a word like *tall* and Johnny doesn't know it, stop. Take time out to teach the family. Teach families whenever you can. They help us remember words and instead of learning one word at a time, we easily learn a whole bunch.

Examples of Word Families

Long *o*	Long *e*	*-all*	*-ay*	*-alk*	*-ou*
go	be	all	away	chalk	around
no	he	ball	bay	stalk	bound
so	me	fall	clay	talk	cloud
	she	mall	day	walk	found
		small	hay		loud
		stall	may		mound
		tall	play		noun
			pray		pound
			say		round
			stay		sound
			way		

What If a Word Can't Be Easily Sounded Out and Has No Word Family?

If the word can't be sounded out and doesn't fit a word family, look for visual patterns and other ways to remember it. For example *want* is a tricky word—it looks like *w-ant* (the insect), but we actually say *w-ont*. Tell Johnny to look out for *w-ant* and pronounce it *w-ont*.

Tricky Words

Some words that aren't easily sounded out and don't fit into word families are *a, because, the, who, want, what, were,* and *you.*

Getting Back to the 10 Words We've Selected

Our mission with these words is to have Johnny practice them over and over again in different ways. Good teachers never teach a thing only once; they teach it many times in different guises, and great teachers make all of them fun. Try these "remember the word" games:

"Remember the Word" Games

- Have Johnny spread out his 10 words face down, then turn them over and read them.
- Do this again, but this time you choose the word to be turned over each time.
- Have Johnny shuffle the words and put them in a pile. Now have him turn each one over and read it out.
- Hold the pack like a fan, facing you. Johnny selects one at a time and reads it out.
- Have Johnny look at the 10 words spread on the table, then shut his eyes while you take one away. Can he name or write the missing word?

- If Johnny turns around three times (or hops, jumps, or claps), then counts to 20, can he still read all the words?

Learning Sight Words Should Be Fun for Johnny

When you use these games, it's up to you to be enthusiastic, fun, and generous with praise. Now's the time to let the performer in you come out!

Have a Game Break, Then Test to See If Johnny Recalls the Words

By now Johnny has had lots of practice in a fun way. Take a break. Play a game for 5 to 10 minutes. When you come back, test Johnny on the words. Have him pick up the pile and read each word to you in any order. Praise him and ask him to point out the most difficult words. How can he remember them? Which letters are hardest? Underline or highlight parts of the word to help him remember it. If a word is really a problem, try writing it down five times, then doing that again twice more during the session.

Sight Words Homework

The 10 words at last go into pocket 1. Johnny's homework is to bring his word folder to you at any spare 5 minutes for testing. Test Johnny by having him pull out his words and read them to you or write them down as you read them out to him. Words go into pocket 2 if they're correct and back into pocket 1 if they're not. Continue doing this once or twice every day until all the words are in pocket 6.

Begin Johnny's next lesson by testing the words from pocket 6. If all 10 words were learned, Johnny colors in (or sticks on) 10 items on his "Words" progress chart. (Progress charts are discussed in Chapter 7.) The completed words go into the big "Done" pocket. If any words from pocket 6 haven't been learned, they go back into pocket 1. If this happens, have Johnny write out the word many times and really encourage him and sympathize. This mustn't become a chore. It should be a chance to succeed and see quick results.

During the next lesson and thereafter, test words from pocket 6 and some random words from the "Done" pocket. You can test them by playing any of the "remember the word" games. Be rapturous about Johnny's mastery of words and set new words each lesson.

Homework Should Be Useful

Remember that homework should be a time to practice skills, not to learn about frustration. Be sure Johnny has had a few trial runs of his homework before being left to work alone. Be prepared to modify the work or abandon it for now if it causes Johnny stress. No homework is worth Johnny becoming despondent.

PART 2 OF A SPRINT LESSON

Phonics

Part 2 of your lesson is where you use worksheets, workbooks, letter cards, or flash cards to teach phonics (sounding out) and spelling. Why phonics and spelling? Because phonics and spelling give Johnny rules. When Johnny hasn't learned to read, he's bombarded by seemingly arbitrary information. He needs to find some order. Phonics and spelling give order to the mess. We will have to teach the hard fact that there are exceptions and irregularities, but even so, phonics and spelling rules clear the fog. Teachers of struggling readers know this, and you'll find tutors and learning centers nearly always emphasize phonics and spelling. So teach phonics and spelling: how to sound out words and recognize frequently occurring letter clusters. See the "Best Resources" section for suggested workbooks.

Spelling Jargon

When we read words by sounding out, it's called *decoding*; when we write words, it's called *encoding*. Adding on to and changing words is called things like *word study* and *word building*.

Different Techniques

A few dyslexia centers use entirely different techniques that include tactile experiences and making 3D models to represent words. They do this in the belief that dyslexics "see" words as pictures and need to manipulate representations of words.

The Spelling Sequence

Phonics and spelling are learned in a sequence. The sequence should be more or less the same in any book you use.

1. Single letter sounds (e.g., *a, buh, cuh*)
2. Short vowel sounds in two- and three-letter words (e.g., h<u>a</u>t, b<u>e</u>t, h<u>i</u>t, h<u>o</u>t, b<u>u</u>n)
3. Double consonant sounds—blends like *st, sm, cl,* and *pr* and the digraphs, *ch, sh, th, ph,* and *wh* in phonetically regular words (*st*op, *sm*ack, *cl*ock, *br*ick, *sh*ed)

4. Long vowel sounds (e.g., m*ee*t, m*ea*t, p*ai*n, p*a*n*e*)

5. More complex letter groupings (e.g., *ight, ought*)

Note: A digraph is two letters that together make one new sound.

Where to Start

Johnny Is a Beginner or Doesn't Know Every Consonant Sound

Start with single sounds and learn them really well. Be especially vigilant with vowel sounds because these are the hardest sounds of all. Make three-letter words as soon as Johnny knows a few single letters (*cat, hat, mat, hen, den, men, pig, big, jig, pot, hot, dot, hug, bug, tug*) so he can hear the vowels in words.

Johnny Reads Three-Letter Words and Some Harder Words, but Erratically

Start by reading phonetically regular words with consonant blends in them, like *stop, spell, skip, black*. Johnny will be reading fairly simple words, but they will look more grown up because of the blends. Johnny may need to revise the blends, but it's usually not blends that give trouble.

Johnny Reads and Writes Fairly Hard Text, but Erratically

The long vowel sounds are a definite trouble spot. This will be the level you start from. But check for competence at the previous levels first. Check that Johnny knows the short vowel sounds, and ask him some of the consonant and double consonant sounds. Revise any he doesn't know and look out for more problem sounds when he reads and writes for you.

Where to Find Books to Teach From

Visit your school resource or reading teacher. Ask what books she recommends and visit school supplies stores as well. Browse before buying, because many phonics books are confusing or too wordy. Here are some common errors:

- A beginning book asks Johnny, "Is this the long or the short sound?" This is hard. It's better to let Johnny master short vowel sounds (*hat, cat, sat, hot, pot, mop*) before starting any long sounds at all.
- Too many written instructions.
- Hard words are included among the easy words, e.g., *well, will,* and *wall*—the *-all* sound should be taught before introducing *wall*.
- Long vowel sounds are introduced without teaching the "magic *e*" and "when vowels go walking" rules.

Good Phonics Books

A good workbook:

- Goes through the sounds in the right sequence:
  - Single letter sounds
  - Short vowel sounds (with no long sounds yet), such as *hat, met, pin, pot, hut*
  - Double consonant sounds, such as *cl, br,* or *st*
  - Long vowel sounds (teaching Johnny the "magic *e*" and "when vowels go walking" rules), such as *bite, beam,* and *steep*
  - Harder sounds (e.g., *ight*)
- Provides fun activities to practice sounds
- Looks appealing to both parent and child
- Has easy-to-follow instructions

For my choices, see the "Best Resources" section.

When Children Start to Read

When children start to read, they must forget the letter names for a while. Always talk of letter *sounds*, not letter names.

c = *kuh*, not *see*
m = *muh*, not *em*

Later you will use letter names again (because the letter name is the letter's long sound).

How to Teach Single Letter Sounds

The best way to teach the letter sounds is to work on three or four letters a week.

- Make a poster or book with things that start with the letter, and keep adding to it.
- Talk about things that start with the letter.
- Find the letter in books or magazines, or on billboards.
- Sing alphabet songs.
- Rhyme and play with sounds.
- Be actively involved!

Programs that turn letters into characters are especially good at helping children remember the letters. Characters are drawn within letter shapes so the letter shape and the sound are learned together. "Zoo-phonics" (www.zoo-phonics.com) is a California program lots of resources teachers like.

Alphabet Songs

Kids usually know the alphabet song (thank goodness for *Sesame Street!*), but try this one too. To the tune of

"Skip to My Lou" and using letter sounds, make up verses like this:

Alice loves apples, *a a a*
Alice loves apples, *a a a*
Alice loves apples, *a a a*
Skip to My Lou, my darling
Bats in the basement, *b b b* . . .
Cathy loves candy, *c c c* . . .

(If Johnny says Keith or Katie; don't worry. It's the sound we want, so we don't have to be too strict.)

Bingo

Kids love games and can learn quickly from kids' bingo and other board or card games. Buy these games from school supplies stores and play them often.

Progressing to Two- and Three-Letter Words (with a Short Vowel Sound)

Johnny can read regular two- and three-letter words as soon as he knows a few letters. The jump from single letters to small regular words is easy. If, for example, Johnny knows *a, t, m, s,* and *c,* he can easily be taught *at, am, cat, sat, mat,* and *Sam.* Remember that vowels have two sounds, long and short (and sometimes three sounds!), and we want to teach only the short vowel sound at first. You can explain that there is a long sound (when it crops up), but concentrate on the short sound for now. Make sure the words you use have the short vowel sound and can be sounded out. Don't, for example, teach *ape,* because the *a* in *ape* is the long sound, and long sounds, being more tricky, are learned later.

Letter Sounds

Short Sound	Long Sound
cat	ape
egg	eve
hit	pile
on	open
cup	clue

MAKE OR BUY A SET OF LETTERS

Have a set of letters for Johnny to make words with. Choose lowercase letters because Johnny will be reading and writing in lowercase and will be taught that capitals are only for the beginning of important names and sentences. Can Johnny make *hat*? *mat*? *hot*? *pot*? Cut out your own letters, handwritten or downloaded from the Internet, or buy a set from a school supplies store. You can get cards, magnetic letters, or tiles for about $5 to $20. Creative Teaching Press (www.creativeteaching.com) has an excellent set of letter cards, called Letter Blocks, for $5. (Make sure you get lowercase.) Whiteboards and blackboards are fun, too.

Teaching Three-Letter Words

Readers read in chunks, not single sounds, so teaching common chunks like *an*, *at*, and *in* helps Johnny avoid having to sound out single letters later. Use lowercase letters, then add onto the front. Example:

This is *an*.
Do you see *a . . . n . . . an*?
Put *c (kuh)* in front: *c . . . an*
It says a new word; it says *can*.

What happens if you take away *c (kuh)* and put *p (puh)* in front?

p . . . an

pan!

What if you put *f* in front?

fan!

Can you make something that I put on my head that ends with *at?*

hat

I wonder if you can tell me a new word if you hide your eyes and I make it when you're not looking.

Can you make a new word while I hide my eyes?

Using Letter Cards to Teach Three-Letter Words

Ask Johnny to make words. Select the letters he needs in advance so he doesn't have to sort through so many. Use this guide:

a words: Use the letters *a, d, g, l, n, p, s, t.*
Make the words *pan, nap, sat, pat, gap, gas, lag, lap, pad, pal, sad, sag,* and *sap.*

i words: Use the letters *d, h, i, n, p, s,* and *t.*
Make the words *pin, win, din, sin, tin, hid, hip, hit, pit, sit, his, dip, sip, tip, dish,* and *ship.*

e words: Use the letters *e, g, l, m, n, p,* and *t.*
Make the words *leg, let, men, met, net, peg, pen, pet, ten,* and *get.*

o words: Use the letters *d, g, h, o, m, p,* and *t.*
Make the words *dog, dot, hop, mop, pod, pot, top, hog, hot,* and *got.*

u words: Use the letters *b*, *d*, *g*, *h*, *m*, *t*, and *u*.
Make the words *bug*, *but*, *hug*, *hut*, *mug*, *tub*, *hum*, *dug*, *tug*, *mud*, *gum*, and *gut*.

Fill-In-the-Vowel Activities

Most beginning workbooks ask Johnny to fill in the missing center vowel in lots of three-letter words. If Johnny doesn't want to do this, put vowel tiles in front of him (or just write the vowels on small squares of paper) and ask him to choose the right one. Write the letter in the workbook for him; later he can read the words back to you.

Flash Cards Are a Great Way to Practice Words You've Started Teaching

Always sort through flash cards before using them. Don't use all the cards at first; instead, use only the words you're teaching. For example, sort out just the regular three-letter words (*hen*, *net*, *box*). A good game is "three for free." Johnny turns over cards from the face-down pile, reads the words, and gets three for free for every three correct cards ("for free" means he doesn't have to read them out). Shuffle each time you play, and Johnny will soon have read all the words. (For good boxes of flash cards, see the "Best Resources" section.)

Real Life: A Lesson in How Not to Use Flash Cards

Sold in their millions, flash cards should come with a warning. It might say: "WARNING: These cards are pointless and tedious unless basic procedures are followed." The following story illustrates this point.

I arrived home from work one day and found my sister Lyn helping my kindergarten child, Lauren, to learn sight words. Lyn had looked through my bookshelves and had come upon a pack of flash cards. The cards were 100 individual sight words. Over the years, my sister had heard me talk many times about the importance of sight words. She had found herself with some spare time that evening and a willing child, and so had thought she would contribute to the learning process. She sat in front of my daughter and held each of the 100 flash cards in front of my daughter's face, one at a time.

"When," said Lyn, holding up the card.

"When," repeated Lauren obligingly.

"Come," said Lyn.

"Come," repeated Lauren.

"Who."

"Who."

"Saw."

"Saw."

"Am."

"Am."

So what was Lyn doing wrong? Why was I dismayed at this apparently fine scene? Because Lauren simply could not learn 100 words, all in one go, by seeing and naming each one after my sister. The task was too enormous. She would probably remember nothing of the session, other than the nice experience of having her aunt interact with her and praise her. Lyn at least knew the importance of praise and had certainly done some good by giving Lauren her attention and encouragement. But as for the learning of sight words, Lauren would have learned nothing.

Lyn had overloaded Lauren. So what should my sister have done?

- *The right amount of information.* Lyn should have selected 5 to 10 cards only. Most of us can retain between 5 and 9 pieces of new information at any one time.
- *Ownership.* So that Lauren felt in charge of her learning, my sister should have invited her to choose her words for herself.
- *Hands-off teaching.* Lauren should have handled the cards herself and put away the remaining cards herself. When you handle the cards, the paper, the book, or whatever is in front of your child, you are taking over. Offer your help, but don't touch unless your child asks you to. If you handle the material, your child immediately feels the work is really yours. Imagine how you would feel if your boss came to your desk and, uninvited, picked up your work. How much better it would have been if you had been given the opportunity to offer your work to her.
- *Learning should be fun.* Lyn should have launched herself, with much enthusiasm, into the business of making the learning fun. Games and changing tempo do this.
- *Praise and encouragement.* Lyn did well on this score. She maintained a flow of praise for each accomplishment.
- *Mastery.* Until children have learned the information they already have, they shouldn't be given lots more. Establish that a group of sight words has been learned before adding more. To test for mastery, Lyn might simply have said,

"I can see you're really good at this. I wonder if you could still tell me the words if you first turned them over so you can't see them, and then mixed them all up. Do you think you could turn each one over and read it?"

She should have been suitably impressed when Lauren correctly identified the words, and if Lauren didn't identify them correctly, she should have saved the offending words for more practice. The words could have been written out a few times, stuck around the house in prominent places and used in "remember the word" games (described earlier in this chapter).

Avoid er, ir, *and* ur

The *er* sound is hard because it's made by all these combinations (*er, ir,* and *ur*). Learn it later as a harder concept. For now, learn the simplest words.

Play Games with the Words to Keep the Fun Going

Here are some examples:

- Cut out pictures from finished workbooks (*bed, pot, hat, cat, dog, mat*) and have Johnny write or stick the right word on each picture.
- Make a pack of cards from the words Johnny knows or buy flash cards, and play the games discussed earlier.
- Write sentences and have Johnny draw pictures to go with them. Make a book. Include silly sentences.

First Sentences for Homemade Books

Mom is big.
Johnny is big.
Daniel is not big.
I love Dad.
I love Mom.
I love Goldie.
I love hot dogs.
I have a cat.

> I have a mom.
> I have a dad.
> I have hats.
> I have pens.
> I have lips.
> I go to school.
> I go to Grandma's.
> I go to bed.
> I go mad!

Double Consonant Sounds

After three-letter words, teach consonant blends like *st, cl, sp,* and *fl* and consonant digraphs like *ch* and *sh*. (A digraph is a pair of letters that makes its own sound.) Teach Johnny to read, write, and make these words using lists or flash cards (see the "Best Resources" section).

Easy Words Made from Consonant Blends

The Blend Is at the Beginning	The Blend Is at the End or the Beginning and the End	The Digraph Is at the Beginning	The Digraph Is at the End
clap	bank	chat	clash
clip	blank	check	ditch
clot	drank	chess	fetch
drip	drink	chick	flash
drop	lost	chimp	flesh

The Blend Is at the Beginning	The Blend Is at the End or the Beginning and the End	The Digraph Is at the Beginning	The Digraph Is at the End
flag	past	chips	mash
flap	plank	chop	match
flat	rest	shed	patch
flip	ring	shot	pitch
flop	sing	shrimp	posh
grab	sink	shut	slash
grip	sting		smash
slip			witch
slit			
slop			
spin			
spit			
spot			
stand			
still			
stop			

The *ch* and *tch* Endings

Notice that the *ch* ending is often preceded by *t*. Make word families to explore this. (You'll find that an *n* is usually followed by *ch*, not by *tch*, for example, *bench* or *inch*.)

nch	*ch*	*tch*
bench	much	catch
bunch	rich	ditch
drench	sandwich	hatch
inch	such	latch
lunch		patch
munch		pitch
wrench		sketch
		witch

Long Vowel Sounds

After double consonant sounds come long vowel sounds. How do we recognize a long vowel sound? There are three common rules for long vowel sounds.

1. When Two Vowels Go Walking, the First One Does the Talking

When vowels come together in pairs, a long sound is made. The first letter of the pair makes its long sound (it shouts out its name!) while the other stays silent.
Examples:

> meet
> meat
> pain
> boat

The pairs of vowels are *ee, ea, ai,* and *oa.*
Examples:

When Two Vowels Go Walking, the First One Does the Talking.

ee	ea	ai	oa
deed	cheat	brain	boast
feed	deal	chain	boat
feel	dream	drain	cloak
feet	each	faint	coast
free	eat	frail	coat
freed	heal	maid	croak
jeep	meat	mail	float
meet	neat	main	load
peep	peach	nail	moat
seed	real	paid	road
sheet	seat	pain	roast
sleep	speak	rail	shoal
sleet	steal	rain	soak
steep	stream	sail	soap
tree	teach	saint	throat
weed	team	sprain	toad
weep	weak	trail	toast

With Spelling Rules, There Are Always Exceptions

Words like *bear, pear,* and *wear* don't follow the two vowels go walking rule, but that doesn't make the rule less valuable. Johnny will be delighted when he can read words because he knows the rule. He won't care too much that there are some exceptions (to learn later).

2. Magic e

When "magic *e*" is on the end of a regular short word like *pin*, the middle vowel changes its sound. The short vowel sound becomes a long vowel sound. *Pin* becomes *pine*. Read the examples and cover over the end *e* to see how magic *e* works. (Some teachers teach "bossy *e*": It makes the vowel shout its name.)

Examples: **"Magic *e*" Words**

Long *a*	Long *e*	Long *i*[*]	Long *o*	Long *u*
blade	compete	bite	bone	brute
cane	complete	dice	chose	cute
cape	Eve	ice	code	flute
fade	Pete	kite	cone	plume
hate	stampede	mice	cope	pollute
made	Steve	nice	home	rule
mane	theme	rice	hope	salute
mate		ride	lobe	
pane		side	mope	
spade		site	pope	
tape		slice	rode	
trade		tide	rope	
vane		twice	slope	
wade		wide	tone	

*Notice the -*ice* family is included among the long *i* words.

> ### *Notice That the Vowel* u *Is the Hardest to Teach*
> The vowel *u* is the hardest to teach because it makes the *uh* sound just like *a* does when it's on its own, as in "a big house."

3. y *Behaving as a Vowel*

This group is often taught with the long vowel group.

- When *y* is on the end of *longer* words, it behaves like an *e* making its long *"EEE"* sound.
- When *y* is on the end of *small* words, it behaves like an *i* making its long *"EYE"* sound.

Examples: *y* **Behaving as a Vowel**

y **Behaving as Long** *e*	*y* **Behaving as Long** *i*
funny	by
happy	my
hungry	pry
silly	shy
smelly	sly

An *ay* on the end of a small word says the long *"AY"* sound. Examples:

ay **Says Long** *a* **Sound**
hay
may
play
say
stay

An *ey* on the end of a word makes the long *"EEE"* sound. Examples:

ey Says Long *e* Sound
honey
key
money
monkey
turkey
valley

Some exceptions are *prey*, *obey*, and *convey*.

One More Nice Little Rule

In these little words, the end vowel is long:

g<u>o</u>, s<u>o</u>, n<u>o</u>
m<u>e</u>, h<u>e</u>, sh<u>e</u>, b<u>e</u>

The noticeable exception here is *to*; we just have to learn the word *to* by sight.

Flash Cards

Easy Vowels and Easy Blends and Digraphs, both published by Frank Schaffer, contain lots of long vowel cards. (See "Best Resources" section.)

More Complex Letter Groupings

This group includes:

- Word endings (*ight, ought, ior*)
- Prefixes (*un-, pre-*)
- Suffixes (*-ent, -ly*)
- Abbreviations (*Mrs., Rd.*)
- Contractions (*can't, won't*)
- Silent letters (*knight, knee*)
- Polysyllabic words and any other complex ways of spelling (*unintentionally, misinformed*)

To Teach Complex Spellings

To teach complex spellings, you should encourage these practices:

- Brainstorming (thinking of lots of examples of similar words)
- Making word families
- Memorizing

Get a workbook that isn't dreary or intimidating!

Always *Give Johnny Scrap Paper and a Pencil When He's Stuck with a Word*

He'll learn to try out a few possibilities and recognize the right version. I call this "practice spelling," and it's the way most of us tackle tricky spellings.

Phonics Homework

The homework for this part of the lesson is to complete an activity or worksheet that practices the sound learned in the session. When each sheet or piece of work is done, the phonics progress chart is filled in.

Remember the spelling sequence:
Single letter sounds:
t, s, l, m, r

Short vowel sounds:
bat, hen, lid, hot, cup (The last two letters are taught as a whole chunk.)

Double consonant sounds (blends and digraphs):
cl, st, br, ch, sh

Long vowel sounds:
hate, pipe (magic *e*)
meet, meat, peel (when two vowels go walking, the first one does the talking)
happy, silly (*y* behaving like long *e*)
cry, shy, my, by, try, why, fry, sly (*y* behaving like long *i*)

Harder letter groups:
fir, fur, her (when *r* is after these vowels, the sound is the same)
presuppose, softly, climb, light (prefixes, suffixes, silent letters, harder word families)

What about Writing?

Because we need the same phonics and spelling skills to write as we need to read, the SPRint program works for writing as well as reading. But when we're encoding (writing) rather than decoding (reading), these modifications help:

- Choose workbooks that require some writing.
- Get handwriting sheets from the teacher and check that Johnny is starting each letter at the right place

and forming each letter correctly. (Many children write badly just because they don't follow the right flow—they're going left when they should be going right, or up when they should be going down. It takes them twice as long to write, and their writing is messy.)

- Teach spelling rules by having Johnny write the words, not just read them.
- Do regular dictation of short paragraphs Johnny has read so he learns to write the words as well as read them. Repeat the same dictation a few times so he can reduce the number of errors each time. Can he achieve perfection in three attempts? Can he do the same dictation perfectly next lesson? Dictation develops correct spelling of familiar words, so silly mistakes are less likely, and encourages the good habit of proofreading.
- Have Johnny do practice spelling, which is described earlier in this chapter.
- Have Johnny proofread, but keep it easy. Instead of demanding that he proofread, try saying something like, "I see two errors, I wonder if you can spot them. Would you like a clue?"

Dictation

Dictation is a great way to consolidate learning. Get sentences from books or sheets you're using and start with single sentences of phonetically regular words. Then progress to short paragraphs:

Easy:
A fat cat had a nap.
Ben fed a red hen.

A big pig sat on a lid.
Dot got a hot pot.
A pup had a run in the sun.

Harder:
The cat ran in the sun and had lots of fun. Then she slept.
Pam got a pet cat. She let it jump on the bed. Mom
was mad.
Dan is big. He put a glass of milk on the top shelf.

PART THREE OF A SPRINT LESSON

Reading

> ### *The Reason We Learn Phonics and Sight Words Is to Read*
>
> Keep this goal in mind, and make sure Johnny gets to read books early on. If all he ever does is learn isolated rules and words, he'll get frustrated.

There's "Reading" and There's "Real Reading"

Learning to read means having good books to read. But what's a good book? If you ask parents of struggling kids and the kids themselves, here's what you'll hear:

> "He can read it all by himself. It's funny. There aren't too many hard words. It's not too long. There's no small writing."

Johnny wants very badly to read, but has been humiliated and frustrated in his efforts before. The best reading books for Johnny are books that are phonetically regulated. Sure, we could give Johnny predictable books he chants out loud. Sure, he could make his own books. These activities are good in lots of ways, but Johnny feels they're not "really reading." Phonetically regulated books are books Johnny can sound out (or decode) for himself, and these must be his first books. (Any parent whose child has flung a book across the room will relate to this!) Get phonetically regulated, fun books so Johnny doesn't have to despair when he meets "too many hard words." Johnny won't come across words he can't read and will build his skills methodically. He'll start with *Big Pig* or *Fat Cat* so he can read the entire book without being dismally thwarted by words like *were*. Guided reading of harder books comes later.

Guided Reading

We've already guided Johnny's reading by improving his fluency (he learned sight words), teaching him to sound out (phonics), and choosing phonetically regulated reading books. We can also guide his reading by correcting his mistakes when he reads aloud to us and by reading aloud with him (called "paired reading").

Here are two ways to correct Johnny's errors when he reads aloud to us:

- Tell Johnny the words he gets wrong, to keep fluency and comprehension.
- Help him work out the words he gets wrong by covering parts of the word so he can sound it out bit by bit.

Here are two ways to read aloud together (paired reading):

- Read aloud with Johnny, slightly in front so he hears your cues or slightly behind so you follow his lead but fill in words when he stumbles.

- Read aloud together by taking turns. Johnny may read the same amount as we do (e.g., a page each) or only a little (selected words or sentences) until he's more confident.

Getting Reading Books

It's vital that Johnny starts to read, but to guarantee success and enjoyment, and so keep him reading, he must start with lots of phonetically regulated books. Allow yourself many visits to libraries, bookstores, and suppliers and see my recommendations in the "Best Resources" section.

The Most Important Thing to Do with Beginning Reading Books

The most important thing to do is to guarantee Johnny's success. Choose simple, phonetically regular books with titles like *Fat Cat* or *Big Pig* to begin with. Make sure you teach any words that can't be sounded out, like *the* and *were*, first. If you show Johnny these words in advance and tell him to watch out for them, he will be able to read the whole book independently. This is really important to struggling kids. They long to be able to do it all by themselves and show you they can. If they come across too many hard words, they'll give up or give you a very hard time!

High-Interest Books with Low-Level Vocabulary

The text of the book mustn't be too difficult or boring. It must have high interest for Johnny but have low-level vocabulary so he's not overwhelmed. Get books that don't have lots of difficult words and are generously illustrated. You want only a few sentences per page and lively themes. Ask teachers and librarians for help. Try to get a collection of books that will last you for several weeks. Phonetically regulated sets are the best. See the "Best Resources" section for suggestions.

Age Appropriateness

It's better to get books that are too easy rather than too hard, but they mustn't make Johnny feel like a baby. Check the text carefully, because he will resent reading *Teddy's Adventures* when he's 8.

What If Johnny Chooses Books That Are Too Hard?

If Johnny chooses a book that's too hard, don't panic. Let him have his choice. Let him use it just for looking at, or offer to read it to him. If you read it often, he'll be able to read parts of it with you later on. Meanwhile, keep selecting phonetically regulated books at the right level of difficulty for him to read for himself.

Reading Together

There are a few ways to read together:

- Read the whole book to Johnny. This is appropriate at any age as long as he enjoys it.
- Read only the first few pages to him so he wants to read a few more pages himself.
- Do paired reading (described earlier in this chapter).
- Have Johnny read or browse while you sit with him reading your own book.

> ### *What about Mistakes in Reading Aloud?*
>
> Correct Johnny's mistakes, but be gracious about it. Simply point to the word (without saying, "No, that's wrong!") and let Johnny correct himself. Cover up parts of the word so Johnny can sound it out bit by bit and look for words within words (such as *un-kind*, *for-get*, or *land-sc-ape*). If the word can't be worked out quickly, give the answer (unless Johnny is the type who *has* to work it out all by himself!). Write the word on a card for practicing in the word folder.

Bedtime Reading

Whichever way you decide to tackle reading, try to include a bedtime reading routine. Building this time into your day is possibly the single most effective strategy you can use. Children need to be given a time for reading because they can't organize this for themselves, and at first would rather do other things. But we won't let them because, in this instance, Mom really knows what's best! Children will come to enjoy this time as long as you are supportive and interested. If siblings share a bedroom and argue, reduce trouble by separating them so each one starts off in a different room. (You can carry little children back to their own bed later.) Each child takes a pile of books to bed and gets 30 minutes to read alone (whether this means reading or just browsing). This time becomes a calming time, and you often find your children are more refreshed in the mornings. They actually needed more restful time than we were giving them. Thirty minutes is not too much, even for little children, as long as they have a selection of books. This is why weekly visits, or more, to the local library are really worthwhile.

Reading Facts

- In the year 2000, 37 percent of fourth-grade students performed below basic reading levels.
- Between 1998 and 2000, the achievement gap in reading between boys and girls increased.
- Explanations of the achievement gap point to interest in subject matter, expectations of sex roles, earlier maturation of girls, and school environment.
- Both men and women view reading as a mostly feminine activity, and their level of education makes no difference to this perception.
- When children start school, their parents soon stop reading aloud to them.
- Boys read far less than girls, but they read over more genres.
- Boys feign confidence at school but actually see themselves as poor readers.

What We Should Do

- Make sure our boys have reading matter they're interested in. Boys read more nonfiction than girls and enjoy "how to" books, sports books, and comics. We should keep reading aloud to boys even after they have started to read themselves. They can enjoy more complex tales this way. (The many Harry Potter and Lemony Snicket stories are favorites.)

- In a boy's early years, when his language skills may be relatively immature, we should talk to him often and include explanations and stories about our own experiences. Baby talk isn't helpful.
- We must try to project positive attitudes about reading and be a reader for boys to see.
- We must involve positive male role models whenever we can.

COMPREHENSION

When Johnny learns the SPRint way:

1. **S**ight words
2. **P**honics
3. **R**eading

he improves his comprehension and writing. But if he needs to improve more, modify your program to include more practice.

- Have Johnny retell stories to practice being clear and concise.
- Read him text in which you substitute nonsense words for real words so he listens carefully to meaning.
- Explain new vocabulary.
- Read or tell well-known stories, but change the endings. Show him books that change traditional tales into funny versions (try *The Stinky Cheese Man* by Jon Scieszka and Lane Smith). He'll learn about changing meanings, using humor, and what does and doesn't make sense.
- Have Johnny reread his books so he's fluent enough to understand the text.

Comprehension

Some people make comprehension just a matter of answering questions after reading text. This makes it boring for children when it needn't be. Books with puzzles and funny text make comprehension fun.

Troubleshooting

Keep Praise and Acknowledgment Constant

Johnny may feign disinterest in your attention, but don't be fooled. All children want to be noticed, loved, and praised by their parents. They want you to be proud of them.

Ask Family and Friends for Help

Our children often go out of their way to be difficult with us. If you can't afford a tutor, but have a great social network, perhaps a grandparent, cousin, or friend could help. You could get books and ideas for them but have them do the face-to-face interaction. (This looks great on college applications, too!)

Help Out

If Johnny's work is scattered all over the house, offer to help him organize it. He'll be grateful, and you'll avoid an unnecessary confrontation. Devise simple rewards and consequences for next time. It's better to keep or restore calm than to insist Johnny lie in the bed he made!

Stay Solution-Oriented

If work isn't done, talk about the work and not about how remiss Johnny is. Say, for example:

"Was the work too difficult this time?"

rather than:

"You don't try hard enough; you never finish anything;
you'll have to try harder."

Offer more help. Reassess rewards to make sure you're still giving ongoing small rewards. Have you lapsed in praising the good things? Even if you're entrenched in an argument, try to get back on track. Acknowledge what you're angry about, but reward effort, too. You might say something like:

"I'm annoyed that you left your homework until too late,
and I want you to be sure to do it tomorrow. One thing
that I've been forgetting to mention, though, is how
well you've been doing at getting ready in the mornings.
You're doing a great job with that."

Special Goals and Rewards for Free

Have a special goal, perhaps a movie or a sleepover, and be enthusiastic about it. Have a free one-off celebration of what Johnny has achieved so far, perhaps a special dinner, ice cream, or an outing. Include things you were going to do anyway. You might say something like:

"Today you've helped me out, so I'm ordering pizza to say
'Thank you.'"

Tell Johnny how well he's doing, what gains he's making, and how proud you are.

When It's All Too Hard, Acknowledge Johnny's Feelings

If Johnny becomes disheartened, acknowledge his feelings. Tell him you understand how hard he's trying and that reading can be a hard nut to crack. Tell him he should be very proud of himself for working hard. Tell him you have faith in him, and know he can see it through. Sometimes, too, it's useful to look at how you give treats. Do you give them randomly? Could you make these same treats contingent on effort? Sometimes parents say progress charts and rewards are difficult for them because their child already gets everything. Try changing this. Tell Johnny you want to reward him for the good things he does that may go unnoticed. You want to make sure you notice all his efforts. Give I'll-play-with-you time, I'll-read-to-you (without your sister!) time, playground time, ice cream, hamburgers, pancakes, trips, play dates, TV time, or video time as rewards. You'll probably end up giving the same things you always have, but now the good things will be linked to Johnny's efforts and successes.

Rest and Food

At the end of the day, children and parents get tired and hungry. This is the time for disputes and difficulties. It sounds obvious, but most parents forget to attend to themselves as well as their children. Taking 30 minutes of quietness, putting your feet up, and having a snack can charge you up to see out the last lap before bedtime. Tell your children this is quiet time, and at bedtime send them to bed early enough to allow them 30 minutes to look at books. An 8 o'clock bedtime is good up to grade 4. You may think this sounds early, but even if Johnny looks fine when he stays up late, he may be tired in school when you can't see him.

Our Comments Are Often Enough Reward

Children can never get enough praise (just like the rest of us!) as long as it's deserved. They know, though, when they don't really deserve praise, and can see when we're overdoing it!

Real Life: Steven Has Everything

Steven loved life. He was 7, and had a new baseball bat, a kitten, an older cousin who visited him often, and a pool table in his room. He couldn't read, but his life was full and happy. He spent long sunny days at play, and his mother, who knew how hard it could be for an only child, made sure he always had enough to do and things to play with. Steven was talkative and full of smiles. He loved to tell me about himself and about all the good things he did. In our lessons, with plenty of games and changes of activity, Steven made good progress.

Steven's mother, Hazel, had one complaint, however: She had trouble getting Steven to do his homework. Each week he came to his lesson with only some of his work done and a note from Mom. The note explained that Steven had thrown tantrums about the work and would not do it, or that the family had been too busy to find enough time for him to do the work. The homework was just too much for Hazel.

Homework can turn our children into whiners and ourselves into nervous wrecks. But there's no avoiding it. When a child's falling behind, he must do homework if he's to make any headway. So, we have to make homework right for him. He has to be able to do it mostly by himself, he must understand it, and it can't be dull or too long. At home, it's important that we provide him with time and a place to do the work, and incentives to keep him going. Steven had everything conspiring against him. A kitten, a cool cousin, a baseball bat—it was hardly surprising he didn't want to do his work! And even if he had wanted to do it, he wasn't able to find a place. He was nearly always out. Hazel had a demanding job and, like most of us, was juggling home and work, and was finding her time and space squashed to nothing. Where was she to find time, or energy, for the homework battle?

Hazel's only choice was to get serious. She knew she had to make a workable plan and minimize interruptions and disturbances. So she specified a time each day for homework. Steven would have a snack when he got in from school, then he would do homework, even on the days he stayed with Grandma. He would not be allowed to promise to do his homework later. Hazel wrote a copy of his schedule for other family members, just to make sure. When Steven was at Grandma's, he was to stick to the homework schedule. Steven's cousin was to come at times that didn't conflict with Steven's homework.

Hazel listed Steven's favorite things and turned them into rewards for doing homework. Instead of just getting play time, it was earned time. The pool table was put to good use by scheduling games with Mom for finished work; there was extra pool time and new treats, too, so that Steven had plenty to look forward to. Not all of Steven's enjoyments were contingent upon his doing his work, but many were. Hazel wrote down a precise plan of what was expected, and Steven knew exactly what the rules were. If Steven completed his homework before the end of the week, then he had extra play time and could call his cousin over. If his homework was not done, then it was done at another time of the week instead of play.

Hazel's campaign worked. She succeeded in getting Steven to do his homework, and she got the whole family used to the new routine. There were still times when things lapsed, but Hazel had never envisaged perfection. She could cope with occasional hiccups because she had the main issue covered. There are very few homework arguments in Hazel's house these days.

IN SHORT

Teach the SPRint way:

1. **S**ight words
2. **P**honics
3. **R**eading

CHAPTER 7

Tutoring Johnny Yourself: How to Teach

THERE ARE TWO PARTS TO READING INSTRUCTION

- What we teach
- How we teach

HOW WE TEACH IS JUST AS IMPORTANT AS WHAT WE TEACH

Boring and disorganized teaching kills Johnny's enthusiasm (and he may never get it back), so we can't leave the "how" part of teaching to chance. There are techniques and styles that work, and we should use them. Essentially, there are three things to remember:

1. Fun and positives
2. Routine and repetition
3. One-step-at-a-time, hands-off instruction

1. FUN AND POSITIVES

Enthusiasm, Support, and Games

Actively plan for Johnny's happiness and success. There isn't a child alive who doesn't want to feel liked and noticed. Be enthusiastic for him. Don't admonish him, and don't be tempted to say things like:

"If you tried harder . . ."
"Put more effort into . . ."
"You should know this . . ."

or similar nagging comments (nag? me?). Be strict with yourself in making this a positives-only domain.

Make sure the important adults in Johnny's life know about his program and will be his supporters. They must praise his successes and never tease him or criticize his efforts.

Make activities short and varied, with games interspersed throughout.

Be prepared to change activities that become stressful, or to play for a while instead of working.

Making Changes When Work Becomes Stressful

If Johnny is uncooperative, ask yourself why. Is it simply that you should be firmer with him? If you think getting firm will work, be sure to tell Johnny the work rules (preferably with his input) and to build rewards into your system. If it's more than a matter of getting firm, think of ways to ease the stress:

- Ask less writing of Johnny. You can write for him while he tells you what to write. If he's in the early stages of writing single letters (e.g., The p_t is hot), provide letter cards so he can show you the letter rather than write it.
- Do easier work for a while before returning to the problem work. (Work with flash cards; make word families; read a joke book.)
- Abandon the particular piece of work. This is far better than having an ongoing battle.

Fun Is More Important Than We Think

It's fun to vary activities and play games, and it makes good educational sense, too. When we have Johnny move, see, hear, touch, and say, we're using multisensory techniques the way the specialists do. It's thought that individual children have dominance in different senses or have different "learning styles," so Johnny may like to see diagrams to understand a concept, while David prefers to listen to you talk about it. This dominance characterizes the two boys, but can change for different tasks. If we engage all the senses when we teach, we give maximum stimulation and provide for the different (and changing) learning styles.

Reward Effort and Success

Organize progress charts. Depending on Johnny's age and temperament, he can make his own or you can make them together. You need a progress chart for each area you teach: sight words, phonics, and reading. Give each progress chart its title (sight words, phonics, or reading), then put 5 groups of 10 items on each chart. The items can be drawn by hand or computer to be checked off, or they can be stickers to put on. Johnny will check off (or stick on) an item each time he finishes a piece of work. For every 10 pieces of completed work, he'll get a reward.

The "Books" Progress Chart

This chart may have fewer items, depending on how quickly Johnny reads the books you select. As the books get harder, he may read (and reread) only one each week.

What Counts as a Reward

Choose rewards before you start work. For a smaller child, pens, stickers, matchbox toys, favorite takeout food, comics, candy, extra TV, later to bed on weekends, and ice cream are good. These smaller prizes are earned after 10 points, and a grand prize is given after 50 points. Grand prizes are things like sleepovers, play dates, outings, videos, movies, or a computer game.

Older boys often prefer to accumulate points without getting small prizes along the way. You can give them a chocolate for every 10 points (just because you're nice!), but the big 50-point prize is usually what they're interested in. Prizes might be sleepovers, meals out, outings, clothes, sports equipment, CDs, DVDs, or computer games.

At the end of a chart, take a break before resuming with a new chart. If your program has become stale, think up new rewards and check that Johnny is being noticed and encouraged by his important adults.

Games

We need games to add fun to our lessons and to give Johnny movement and a change of pace. He will be able to work better after a game break. Games should last 5 to 10 minutes and should follow 15 to 30 minutes of work, depending on Johnny's age and nature.

Playing Cards

Playing cards are the easiest games to find. You can adapt any child's game like Fish, Donkey, or Old Maid so it lasts only 5 or 10 minutes. When you play, be sure to ham up your performance to provide more fun. Children love it when you're always getting beaten or you complain about their superior skill!

Make Your Own Educational Cards

If you know some popular card games like Old Maid and Fish, and feel creative, make your own versions using letters of the alphabet or sight words.

Wacky cards is a fun homemade card game. Add three to six "wacky" cards (cards with the word *Wacky* written on them) to a pile of letters or words that you've made (index cards work fine). Put the pile face down, and take turns turning the cards over and reading them. When a wacky card is drawn, the drawer does a wacky movement (he pinches his nose and says "honk honk," knocks on the door, stands up and down five times, for example).

Games with Shooting Targets

These games provide lots of movement. Flicking or throwing things is a favorite activity. Throw balls into a bucket; shoot balls into a hoop; throw coins into a muffin tray (put numbers in each cup and add up your score); throw plastic Easter eggs into a hat. Let Johnny win most of the time, but make it close!

Darts and Pool

These are much-loved games. Work out a way to have shots for 5 or 10 minutes with some sort of challenge or objective (like being the first to score 100).

Construction Games or Puzzles

Games of this type can be good. Some children love being timed with a stopwatch, but be sure to make the time one they can achieve. You can write down the time score and have Johnny try to beat it next time. As always, be lavish with praise.

Paper and Pen Games

These games are easy. My favorite is "Boxes." Have Johnny draw 4 rows of 4 dots, making a grid of 16 dots. A turn is when you draw a line vertically or horizontally between 2 dots. (You can't go diagonally.) Players take turns until one player makes a box. This person puts his initial in the box and gets another turn. Keep going until all 9 boxes have been made and count up who has the most boxes. A good variation is to give Johnny five spellings to start the game. He must write the spelling, and for each word he spells correctly, he gets a turn but you don't! After the five spellings, you start to play too.

Boxes Game

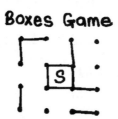

Board Games

Board games like Chutes and Ladders, checkers, and tic-tac-toe are lots of fun. Give yourself a handicap like missing the first three turns or allowing your opponent to double every 6 he throws. Maybe he can double his 6 if he reads or spells a word. Make sure the game can be played in 10 minutes.

Hide the Word

This game is great for younger children. One of you hides a card with the word on it somewhere in the room, and the other finds it. The hider guides the finder to the card by saying:

"You're getting hotter" (when the finder moves closer to the hidden word).

"You're getting colder" (when the finder moves farther away from the hidden word).

The finder reads out the word when he has found it. (A nice variant on this is to hide the word, with a jelly bean, inside a plastic Easter egg.)

2. ROUTINE AND REPETITION

Same Time, Same Place, Same Order

Establish a routine quickly:

- Have lessons at the same time each week. (A 1-hour lesson once or twice each week is good.)
- Run lessons at the same distraction-free place.
- Always have good pencils and paper at hand.
- Always teach the three SPRint activities, sight words, phonics, and reading, in the same order. If you change the order, tell Johnny what you're doing. Some kids fret about change, any change, but even if Johnny's not that type, it's nice to keep him informed (it's really his show, after all!).
- Always give homework at the end.
- Always include games and rewards.

Same Thing Presented in Different Ways

Sight words get remembered when we practice them in different ways. To teach new sight words, do some or all of the following:

Activity 1

- Copy five words on a piece of paper.
- Look at the words, fold the paper to hide them, and write them from memory.

- Open the paper and check the words.
- Do the folding activity twice more with the same paper, so it gets smaller.

Activity 2

- Write the words neatly, cut out each word, turn the words face down, then turn each one over and read it out.
- Mix the words up and do this again.

Activity 3

- Hide the words around the room for your partner to find (and vice versa).

Activity 4

- See how many of the words can be found in a page of writing.

Activity 5

- Make giant copies of the words and tape them to the wall.

A Note about How We Remember Things

- The things we remember are of two types:

  Small pieces of information stored in short-term memory (STM)

  Larger pieces of information stored in long-term memory (LTM)

- When sight words are first learned, they go into short-term memory. Information stored in short-term memory can be stored for only a short time, and only in small amounts. We can store only five to nine new things in short-term memory at any one time, so this number of sight words should be given.

- If we want to keep information longer (or remember more), it has to go to long-term memory. To do that, we attach meaning to it. Think of the memory devices we typically use:

Every Good Boy Deserves Fruit, to remember music notes

Richard Of York Gave Battle In Vain, to remember the colors of the rainbow

My Very Excellent Mother Just Showed Us Nine Planets, to recall the sequence of planets

- Lots of information finds its way into LTM, and we must see that sight words make their way into Johnny's LTM. To do this, we help Johnny attach meaning to words as quickly as possible. Meaning comes as words are read in context, and sometimes we can get meaning from drawing attention to the shape or pattern of words. We can make visual groups, like *hitting shopping pulling hopping*, to help Johnny remember shapes and patterns. Also, we can improve recall by anchoring new information to what Johnny already knows. Johnny knows *all*, so now he learns *small, tall, ball*, and *fall*.

- Teach five to nine new items, repeat them often, and attach meaning soon.

3. ONE-STEP-AT-A-TIME, HANDS-OFF INSTRUCTION

Ownership

Ownership of work is something many teachers overlook or discount. Some teachers habitually interfere with children's work, never noticing the subtle impact of their intrusion. No one likes to have his things tampered with, without having given consent. Everyone enjoys doing things for himself. When we teach, a hands-off approach is best. Provide choices and help, but never take over. Let Johnny do his own work; don't be tempted to control it. Children lose interest if you take over. They may not be able to tell you you've stolen their show, but they feel it. Let them hold the pen, the paper, the book; let them make choices. Offer suggestions when they want you to, but stop offering suggestions as soon as you can. Back off. Be there strictly as a facilitator.

Real Life: The Computer Teacher Who Commandeered His Student's Work

Carol took a course to learn simple computer use. She wanted to be able to help her children and to feel she understood the general flow of everyday conversations. She knew technology had passed her in a quick rush. In her class, she learned how to keep files, save her work, and understand terms like *hard drive*, *floppies*, *RAM*, *ROM*, and *disk burning*. She loved her classes, and knew her efforts would be worthwhile.

One day she got stuck. She couldn't figure out how to fix the mess she had made of her work. She called the teacher over. Mr. Harrison began to tap at the keyboard. His brow furrowed, and he became absorbed in the problem. Tap, tap, tap went the keys. Mr. Harrison called over Mr. Evans, his co-teacher. They discussed things Carol had never heard of. By this time she was standing behind her teachers, who were talking and tapping and bringing up new screens. After 5 minutes, the problem was solved.

"There you are," said Mr. Harrison. "Problem solved."

"What did you do?" asked Carol.

"Oh, don't worry, it's all a bit technical," said a satisfied Mr. Harrison.

Carol continued her work. But she felt, for the first time, that she didn't know much at all. She didn't feel enthusiastic about that piece of work anymore. When Carol got home, her family heard none of her usual chatter about that day's class.

Real Life: The Teacher Who Criticized without Due Care

Marie, aged 15, wanted a part-time job. She wasn't so good at writing letters, so she took her job application to a teacher to proofread. The teacher scanned the letter and got out her pen. After 5 minutes, she handed the letter back to Marie. She had put a line straight across the page. The letter was completely rewritten. Marie couldn't help the look on her face. How could the teacher have done such a thing? Her letter surely wasn't that bad; she had only needed a basic spelling and punctuation check, with perhaps some minor alterations. Did the teacher think she was a complete idiot? Was she too stupid for a real job? Marie brooded about the letter for days. It knocked her confidence. She never felt the same toward that teacher again, and she didn't mail her application.

Task Analysis

Task analysis is taking things one step at a time. When good teachers plan their activities, they break each one into easy progressive steps. Everything can be broken down like this, but some people do it better than others. Start by writing down the steps you will teach, then look again to see if a step can be broken down more and made simpler and clearer. Make sure you're starting from the very beginning and not partway through a process. Make sure you've included every step and put things in the shortest, simplest way you can. Apply task analysis to tasks you teach and instructions you give, too, especially with younger children. Tell them the first thing they must do, then the next, and so on. Use simple phrases and give no more than three instructions at a time. Children can't recall long lists of instructions, and people who give long, complicated instructions often think children are being obstructive, when in fact they just haven't understood.

Real Life: The Compass

I recently attended an excellent "train the trainer" outdoor education program. The program was for a whole day and gave wonderful examples of good teaching. Participants were given plenty of changes of activity, lots of hands-on involvement, and lots of good outdoor food, too. The trainers knew how to make their subject lively and absorbing.

One of the skills the trainers showed was teaching children to use a compass. They took small groups of us and taught us as if we were children. This was a good technique because we got to "walk through" the activity. It's always better to do, rather than listen, if an activity lends itself to doing. So we all used the compass, and the teacher skillfully guided us through each step.

When it was our turn to practice without our guide, we were put in pairs and told to teach our partner as if she were a child. Again this was teaching at its best because repetition and practice are effective ways to consolidate learning. I turned to my partner and offered myself as her pretend child. Without preliminaries, my partner said to me,

"You look at 120 degrees, and you face that way."

Like me, she had just heard and experienced the right way to do it. She had just been the "child" herself and had been taught by a good trainer! But even so, she launched straight into what should have been the last part of the learning sequence. This person was just not used to teaching. Unless you have experience, you tend to launch into the end stages of a whole sequence of instructions. You don't break up your task. You don't start at the beginning. So what should my partner have started with?

"This is a compass. We use a compass for finding our way around. It looks a bit like other things you will have seen, like a stopwatch, for example. But it doesn't tell any sort of time; it's only for finding our way around. The way it helps us to find our way around is by showing us the four direction points. You will often see the four directions on a map. You see a cross, and at the top point there is an N. Do you know what the N means? Do you see the N on your compass? What are the other three points? Can everyone see them? (Help the person next to you if she can't see them.) Very good. Now, what's the right way to hold the compass? Can we ever hold it any other way?"

This is how task analysis works. Teach one simple concept at a time. Give opportunities to practice at each stage. Build up to the harder levels of understanding. Become proficient at task analysis (but up-tempo too; you have to be multiskilled!) and children will never become lost or disheartened.

IN SHORT

Our teaching should emphasize:

- Fun and positives
- Routine and repetition
- One-step-at-a-time, hands-off instruction

4

The Fourth Way: Turn Pointless Homework into Homework with Every Point

To make a difference, we must:

- Accept that Johnny will probably need our help every night.
- Help him organize his homework and his schoolbag.
- Have the teacher modify Johnny's work if he needs it (or modify ourselves).

CHAPTER 8

Homework

GIVING HELP EACH NIGHT

When Johnny isn't doing well with his homework, he needs our consistent, directed, and frequent help. We must help him every night with the things that cause the problems. Is it that Johnny forgets to bring work home? Is it that he doesn't understand the homework instructions? Is it that he simply feels overwhelmed?

Ways Parents Can Help

- Have a clear and strictly enforced homework routine.
- Provide a distraction-free, properly equipped place for Johnny to work.
- Check through Johnny's bag and folder each night and help him get rid of finished work. Organize Johnny's notes and assignments with him, and have him do progressively more of this for himself.
- Check Johnny's homework diary each night and praise him when he puts entries in it.
- Insist that schoolbags and all easily lost items are put in their right place.
- Have checklists.
- Have a system for getting assistance.

Systems for Getting Assistance

When Johnny does his homework, we should sit next to him to help throughout, if he wants us to, or be nearby and ready to come when he calls. We have to help him quickly, before frustration sets in. When we can't help—perhaps Johnny's forgotten to bring home some instructions—we need a school buddy. Try to have the phone number of a reliable classmate Johnny can call in times of need. Although it's rather mercenary, cultivating friendships with helpful kids can give Johnny a safety net.

Did You Know?

The average child watches over 3 hours of TV every day, and 52 percent of children between the ages of 5 and 17 have a TV in their bedroom. If the TV disrupts your homework plans, establish separate times for each. Tape favorite TV programs to watch after homework's done.

Children with Reading Difficulties May Be More Easily Distracted Than Their Friends

A study of how children do their homework found that students with learning disabilities engaged in practices that interfered with homework completion to a greater extent than other children. In other words, they wasted time instead of doing their homework!

Another recent study found that a child's ability to ignore visual distractions and get work done depends on "the availability of working memory." In other words, if Johnny uses up all his working memory to read, he hasn't got enough left to block out the mail arriving or the phone ringing. He can't help being distracted and driving us crazy!

Helping Johnny Organize His Work and His Bag

It's easy for us to think Johnny should be responsible for organizing and doing his own homework. We don't recall our own parents helping us so much, and besides, we want Johnny to learn responsibility. The trouble is, though, kids these days do much more sophisticated homework than we did. At 9 years old, Johnny will be asked to submit, within a time frame, typed reports with bibliographies! Johnny really can't do his homework all by himself, and most parents confess to spending hours helping their children with homework. They don't do it because they've hours of free time on their hands, or because they're mad keen to take part, but because their child will be disadvantaged if they don't.

Homework Must Be Modified for Children Who Struggle with Reading

If Johnny has reading difficulties, he may not be able to do the same type or amount of homework as his peers. If you feel Johnny's homework should be modified, ask, in a reasonable tone, that specific modifications be made. Assure the classroom teacher of Johnny's willingness to oblige, under the right circumstances. It may sound like a lot to ask, but simple modifications can always be made, and a lot is at stake.

Types of Modifications

- *Written instructions.* Ideally, we want clear, well-spaced, short sentences, perhaps enlarged. In reality, instructions can be lengthy, confusing, and badly printed. If Johnny can't read homework instructions, you can read them for him, but in class he'll need other help. Can a buddy read to him? Can the teacher or a buddy help him highlight key words?

- *Alternatives.* In place of writing, Johnny should be allowed to use diagrams, cutouts, drawings, or anything else that will pad out his work and make him feel he's produced enough. His written homework should be limited to a realistic amount.
- *Helping strategies.* Johnny can dictate his work for you to type; he can have a classroom buddy and a homework buddy to phone if instructions get forgotten; he can have another child be the "checker" who checks that he has his homework sheets and has handed in the sheets that are due. Ask Johnny's teacher for good ideas.

Real Life: Teachers Can Work with You to Make Homework Better

When 9-year-old Richard dropped his bag on the kitchen table, his mother searched for homework. If she found any, the tone of the evening was set. She would nag Richard to do it, he would complain that he didn't know how, then she would try to figure it out for herself. Often she wouldn't understand the homework, and, just like Richard, she'd feel like hurling it across the room. Didn't the teacher know she had set them up? Why couldn't she give Richard homework he could manage?

Evenings in Richard's house were filled with anxiety and frustration, and homework kept being sent home. In the end, Richard started taking his homework back to school without ever having taken it from his bag. His teacher didn't complain, and the pointless routine continued. Richard's mom contacted me and asked, in particular, for help with homework. I arranged to meet Richard's teacher.

When I went to Richard's school, I was wondering what his teacher could be like. How could she ignore Richard's difficulties? Would I be able to suggest we look at the homework problem together? Would she be set in bad ways?

Mrs. Wentworth turned out to be just what I hadn't expected. She was friendly, obliging, and very concerned about Richard. But, she said, he received no extra help at school, and needed so much that she just couldn't fill the gap. She knew the homework was pointless, but didn't expect him to complete it, just to go through the motions. She had thought she was sparing his dignity by sending it home. She was delighted that I was taking on the job, and she was happy to discontinue giving Richard homework, since I would use the SPRint program, and its homework, with him. She offered to help in any way she could.

Richard did the SPRint program with me for 8 months. He improved, gained confidence, and even reversed the usual homework equation: He took his homework *to* school to do when the classwork was too hard. Mrs. Wentworth, happy with this system, rewarded his application and improvement.

After a bad start, homework worked for Richard at last. But it took consistent and systematic help with reading and some simple modifications in class.

Real Life: Solutions, Not Blame

"I haven't given my work in," wailed 8-year-old Sam. "Mrs. Shultz will tell me off in front of the whole class. She always does. I'm dumb. I can't do anything right."

Jenny, Sam's mom, had just pulled some tattered worksheets from Sam's overstuffed bag. The worksheets were completed, but hadn't been handed in. She was annoyed because Sam was behind in giving his work in and was supposed to be making a big effort. Jenny had written Sam little reminder notes, had talked about being tidy and writing things down as soon as they came to mind, and had given him checklists. She was exasperated to find the mangled worksheets, but what more could she do?

That night, Sam cried, and Jenny felt like crying too. Sam wished out loud that he could wake up to find it had all been a bad dream. That he was really smart and organized and had a kind teacher. Jenny promised him the next day off school. She told Sam they needed to sort out the school mess together after a good night's sleep. Jenny left Sam sniffling into his pillow and poured herself a drink.

"Just what are they doing at school?" Jenny said to her husband, Tim. "Are late papers worth this torment? I wanted my child to love school and be secure and happy. Now I have a nervous wreck on my hands."

Tim listened to Jenny and replied, "It will all look different tomorrow, Jen. You'll work it out, honey; you're always great at things like this."

Jenny was mildly comforted by Tim's words, but her anger simmered all night.

The next day she dropped her youngest son at school and went to see Sam's teacher. She had a plan. She told Mrs. Schultz that Sam was sick today, but was going to attack the missing homework. She asked if she could have Sam's overdue worksheets, and she asked to see Sam's desk. Mrs. Schultz showed Jenny Sam's desk, and Jenny had to look twice. Crumpled papers were overflowing from every shelf. The contents were jammed in solid. The desk was a disaster area, and a few other desks in the row looked just the same. Jenny was stunned. She pulled out an armful of papers and saw Sam's reading workbook. She extracted it and returned the other papers to the desk. Mrs. Schultz started talking about how far behind Sam was and how he really needed to do such and such a paper to understand what was going on in class. Jenny smiled and replied, "We're really going to tackle this backlog, but I feel that right now we may only be able to manage what is required for grading. I want to help

Sam work on bite-sized pieces of the problem, so could you give me just the crucial papers for now? We'll work on this today with a superhuman effort!"

All that day Jenny worked with Sam. She made sure Sam understood his work, typed his reading project while he dictated, and made him throw out excess papers. She took a load off Sam's back, and the work of several weeks was done with minimum stress. Sam looked at his pile of work, inside a clean new manila folder, and smiled broadly at last. Jenny felt she had really helped for once. She had "chilled out" a little. Her day off work had been worthwhile. There was no berating or nagging, just step-by-step solutions. When Jenny collected little Paul from school, she went back to see Mrs. Shultz. She handed over the work, then headed for Sam's desk. She pulled the entire mass of papers onto the floor and smiled up at Mrs. Schultz.

"Do you think you could help me sort this, Mrs. Schultz? You know how kids won't throw anything out, so I'll take matters into my own hands. I'll do a quick spring clean, and I'm sure Sam will be able to find things better."

Mrs. Schultz worked with Jenny for 15 minutes. They found several completed papers that Sam hadn't handed in. They made a substantial pile for recycling. Jenny was pleased, and Mrs. Schultz looked satisfied too. Jenny made no comment about the mess of most of the desks, and she didn't comment on the mess she had found in Sam's book. She wanted to say, "Can't you get the kids to tidy their desks? Can't you get them to write a little work legibly instead of a mountain of work all scrawled in disarray?" but she didn't. Jenny felt that if Sam was to survive this school year, small bites were best. This year would be a lesson in finding solutions. Jenny headed for her car and thought of another strategy on her way: She would ask Colin, Sam's friend at school, to remind Sam each day to check his bag before leaving class.

She'd offer a small reward! By the time Jenny drove off, she was singing to herself and thinking that, just as Tim had said, things really do look better the next day.

IN SHORT

- Struggling children may need our help every night.
- We can help by having practical strategies, like a strictly enforced homework routine, good work conditions, and a list of helpers to call on (usually Johnny's friends).
- Overwhelming, too-hard homework should be modified to meet Johnny's needs. We can ask the teacher to help in ways like accepting diagrams, cutouts, or other such material instead of writing and giving Johnny a classroom buddy who can explain complex writing.

PART **5**

The Fifth Way: Guide Johnny Safely through "Boy Issues"

Although we do our best to even the pitch between boys and girls in school, boys get into more trouble and often stay in trouble. To keep Johnny safe, we must focus on solutions, not blame. Instead of a "bad boy" label, we need strategies that turn bad situations around.

CHAPTER 9

Boy Issues

Boy Facts

- Boys receive disciplinary action in school far more often than girls.
- Boys call out in class, invited or not, eight times more often than girls.
- Boys score lower than girls on national literacy tests.
- Boys have learning disabilities in slightly larger numbers than girls but are identified as having learning disabilities about three times as often because of their more boisterous behavior.
- Mothers often describe their sons as less communicative than their daughters.
- Adults tend to treat boys more harshly than girls.
- Boys are more physical than girls.
- Boys are often said to be more competitive than girls.
- More boys than girls are involved in violence and carry guns.
- About half the young adults with criminal records or a history of substance abuse (mostly boys) have reading difficulties.

NIPPING TROUBLE IN THE BUD

Whether schools make things hard for boys or brain differences and surges of testosterone act against them, the results are the same: Boys get into trouble. What can we do? We can arrange play dates to help Johnny with friendships; sign him up for sports and clubs so he has fun; work consistently on his reading so he improves in class. We can combat the "bad boy" label by focusing, with the teacher, on solutions, not blame.

Real Life: A "Bad Boy" Label Masks Reading Problems

I was lucky enough to work in a great high school for several years. I directed a unit for students with learning difficulties, and my job was primarily to teach reading.

One day I was summoned to the vice principal's office. He had a favor to ask. He realized that the kids I was teaching should be the ones with considerable reading difficulties, but there was one child, Chris, who was causing problems. This child walked out of class and was a regular clown. He got classes hyped up, and the teachers were sick of it. Could I take him?

When Chris came to our class, the kids were ecstatic. Not only was Chris a pleasant change, but he was super cool. He was a well-known "dude," and he mixed with regular kids. Chris strutted into class, announcing that the kids shouldn't get too excited: They were lucky to have him, and he might not stay long. He chose his seat, proudly relinquished by its former occupant, and settled into some antics. The kids asked him questions, and he delighted them with his clowning. Everyone was happy.

On that first day, the kids explained our reward system to Chris: the everyday rewards and the big excursion we worked all semester for. They showed him our games, boasted that our class was cool, and hoped Chris would show up the next day. He did.

He came and went, and I cleared this with the principal, asking him to give me a week to induct Chris. I told Chris he had to decide whether to join our class. If he joined us, he would have to stay in class and not leave, and he would have to be patient about getting my attention. The other kids' reading difficulties would demand my time, and when that happened he would have to work independently. I told him we could be friends, but I would expect him to abide by the rules. Chris listened with a great show of seriousness and maturity and announced that it seemed like a pretty cool system. One thing, though: How could we deal with the problem of having two people named Chris in the class? I suggested that we call our newcomer by his initials, CJ. The name was an instant success, and within days everyone was calling Chris CJ. He decided to become a full-fledged member of our little class!

Twelve-year-old CJ was the school clown. No one really expected much of him; they just hoped he would stay out of serious trouble. But CJ surprised everyone. He rose to the role of classroom expert in our class and improved in all his outside classes while still holding on to his "dude" status. But CJ did have reading difficulties that had been masked by his trying behavior. He was a clown because he had been getting ever more disheartened and bored by work that was too hard. He improved in our class simply because he could manage the work that was asked of him. I last heard that CJ, still called CJ, works in his uncle's butcher shop. I have no doubt he's a favorite with the customers.

Real Life: Tom—Held Back by a Label

Tom could read, but was practically unable to write. He had good fine motor skills and normal vision and hearing, but consistently produced only one or two muddled sentences each lesson. His mom, Kate, a lawyer, couldn't understand why he had this specific learning block. She asked me to meet her.

Tom, she said, was having trouble accepting his parents' recent divorce. His best friend had just moved away, too, so he was rather adrift and was seeing a psychologist to help him adjust. At school Tom showed no signs of anxiety, but seemed to be stuck with this difficulty with writing. He was making no progress, so Kate wanted me to work on his writing.

Tom and I hit it off from the first. He was an avid talker and gave colorful and humorous accounts of school and life in general. He was something of a showman, and demonstrated things he was learning in private drama lessons. He could mimic, ham up stories, and tie his thin body into impossible-looking knots. He was altogether an entertaining and charming child. Tom did the SPRint program willingly, loved our games, and always did the homework I set. Like many of us, Tom was lively and restless and needed to expend energy, but he was able to work for an hour as long as we took movement breaks.

In week 2, I took a careful look at how Tom wrote his letters, and his problem jumped right out at me. Tom had developed a habit of writing most of his letters in his own topsy-turvy style. He started letters at the wrong point and formed them in awkward turns that didn't allow him to write smoothly and continuously. Once I pointed this out to him, he had only to form new habits. We started by writing the single letters with the right movements and quickly progressed to sentences. I tapped his arm at every error and made grimaces and exaggerated moans. We had fun, and Tom wasn't daunted or embarrassed by the process. Once he could form letters fluidly and knew more spellings (because of the SPRint program), his writing was transformed. He produced more and better work, and Kate showed me samples of work that looked nothing like his earlier pieces.

So why had Tom been so stuck? I came to understand his difficulties in a new way when I bumped into his classroom teacher one day.

I was collecting my own child from her child-care center when Tom's teacher unexpectedly approached me. Her child attended the same center, and she had recognized me. She commented on the progress Tom was making, then said, "You do know he has emotional difficulties, don't you? He sees a psychologist; he's not your normal child. I've known him a long time now, and he has real problems."

And what problems poor Tom must have had! This teacher was in effect absolving herself from responsibility by labeling Tom. She could not be held responsible for Tom's lack of progress with writing because Tom had emotional problems. How could she be expected to change an inherently unchangeable child?

Luckily for Tom, he continued to make such obvious progress that his teacher was happy to have been wrong. She encouraged him and said that of course she had known all along that he simply needed some focused, one-on-one instruction! By the end of the grade, Tom was completing the same written work as his peers.

Don't Let Johnny Be Labeled

For a while Tom's teacher had mentally stuck a label on his forehead saying, "Emotionally disturbed; cannot be helped." This type of labeling is bad for everyone. If you aren't happy with Johnny's progress, don't get stuck in negative opinions. Focus on what Johnny can do and what will help him read and write.

Expect the Best from Johnny

If Johnny is getting into trouble in school, try not to get bogged down in the bad things. Look for the good things, and try to project to Johnny the impression that you expect good things from him (even though you actually feel like screaming at him!). Move on quickly from difficult incidents. Let the teacher know you have faith in Johnny (yes, faith). Sometimes teachers may be looking only at Johnny's bad behavior, so you need to redirect their attention to solutions you can both work on. Don't let negative people shower you with blame, either. It's never productive to stay stuck in a blaming mode. Move forward. Find strategies. Aim to support Johnny, and have confidence in his better nature. Remember, you need solutions, not (definitely not) blame.

The Self-Fulfilling Prophecy

The notion of the "self-fulfilling prophecy" was first documented in 1968. Two psychologists, Rosenthal and Jacobson, wrote "Pygmalion in the Classroom," a description of a classroom based psychology experiment. In their experiment, the psychologists told a classroom teacher they had found, from tests, that some of her students were in fact gifted. They led her to believe that these students were capable of exceptional work, and they studied what effect, if any, this had on the children's performance. Their findings led them to describe the self-fulfilling prophecy.

After testing the children, observing the class, and talking with the teacher, Rosenthal and Jacobson concluded that the teacher's expectations gave rise to commensurate behavior in the children. When the teacher thought a group of children was exceptional, she conveyed this, and those students adopted the same belief and began to excel in their academic achievement. Conversely, when she expected little of her students, they achieved little.

Since that first groundbreaking experiment, research has continued to tell us that social learning is always evident in the classroom. Researchers urge that their findings be incorporated into teacher training courses. They are still finding, all these years after the self-fulfilling prophecy was identified, that while teachers are generally correct in their judgments of what each child needs, unconscious biases or treatment of particular children can lead to a self-fulfilling prophecy.

Boys Are Overrepresented among Children Thought to Have ADHD (Attention Deficit Hyperactivity Disorder)

Boys are diagnosed with ADHD many times more often than girls. Is this an epidemic of negative labeling? Some doctors feel it may be. They say that boys who are identified as having ADHD may just be lively boys who are forced into inactive and restrictive modern-day lifestyles. If Johnny is diagnosed with ADHD, we must decide whether we agree with the diagnosis and whether we want Johnny to take drugs. If we choose drugs, most professionals now urge us to learn new parenting skills too.

Real Life: Is It or Isn't It ADHD?

Paul and Lisa ran a successful business and worked hard. They had two children, Mark and Daniel, and a full-time baby-sitter. The children loved their baby-sitter, and the family flourished.

When Mark was 4, the baby-sitter resigned, and everything changed. Mark became antagonistic and unruly with Lisa. He threw tantrums, hit and kicked her, and couldn't be appeased. She tried spanking, time-out, and bribery, but nothing worked.

When Mark was 6, he was intermittently on "daily report" at school. His behavior was talked about among family friends. Mark had walked over the top of a table at a restaurant; he had purposely tipped a bottle of soda onto the dining room carpet; he had broken Lisa's finger when he pushed past her through a doorway. Lisa read about ADHD and visited a doctor. The doctor prescribed Ritalin. Mark took his "rash" pills for a year, but when he was 7, decided his rash wasn't so bad and he didn't want to take the pills. After that, Lisa crushed the pills into Mark's food, and things went OK for another 2 years. Then somehow the kids at school found out and started telling Mark he was taking "crazy" pills. Mark started to watch Lisa when she prepared his food, and she had to find ever more creative ways to get the pills past Mark's lips. But then Lisa announced that she was buckling under the strain of raising Mark. She said Paul gave her no support. A few weeks later, she left Paul and the boys.

Paul asked Lisa to reconsider, but she never went back to him and gave him custody of the children. Paul, bitter with Lisa, reversed as many of her decisions as he could. He sold the house. He took Mark off his pills.

How did Mark cope? Did his behavior change? Could his dad control him? Mark did not act up for his father and stopped misbehaving in school. The transition from medication to nonmedication was not really noticed amidst the general mayhem, and Paul now maintained that Mark had never had ADHD, just a weak mom. But whether Mark had had ADHD or was just badly managed, he had taken Ritalin for nearly 4 years. The long-term effects of using Ritalin aren't yet clear.

Putting a Dad Slant on ADD

Steve Biddulph, child psychologist and parenting author, says that while ADD (Attention Deficit Disorder) is a real problem for many boys, for some who lack support from adult males the problem isn't Attention Deficit Disorder at all, but "Dad Deficiency Disorder."

Real Life: Andrea's Sons

When I was writing this book, I met a mother, Andrea, who was home-schooling her three boys. She told me about the difficulties she had had when her boys attended regular school. Andrea's first son, Harry, had been diagnosed with ADHD. He was giving his teacher problems, so Andrea went to many meetings at school and seemed to be always responding to claims that Harry was unruly. Harry's teacher advised Andrea to consider medicating Harry for his ADHD.

Andrea felt despondent. The whole family was becoming stressed and upset, but Andrea couldn't accept what seemed to her a brutal reaction. She felt there must be other ways to help Harry. On the advice of a psychologist, she attended parenting classes to see if they could help her control Harry's too lively behavior. The classes were helpful, and Andrea began to feel more confident. But the comments from school were still deflating. After much thought, Andrea decided she had lost faith in the school system. She gathered a pile of work and started home-schooling all three boys.

Andrea decided to make her teaching active and flexible. When I met her, she and her boys were staying at a campsite for several weeks. She was teaching the boys ecology and environmental protection, and told me that all three had finished the prescribed coursework early and were doing extra enrichment work intended for gifted children. Andrea seemed happy. She said she was using a reward system for behavior management and Harry's behavior had improved considerably. While her children were not angels, and at times she lamented the decision she had made, she was mostly glad she had chosen this road. Her boys were lively, happy, and accomplished, and, best of all, she felt empowered and optimistic.

Andrea's children played with mine for 4 days. There were no problems and only typical children's skirmishes. If Andrea hadn't told me her story, I couldn't have distinguished Harry from the rest of the boisterous crowd.

Bad Behavior Can Mask Reading Difficulties

Unless children have major emotional or behavioral problems, they can settle down when they're given work at their level in a happy and supportive environment. If you know Johnny behaves badly in school and think he may have reading difficulties, ask the teacher what's being done for him. Schedule a meeting to discuss ways to help him. Be sure to get specific strategies from the meeting and list them on paper. Schedule another meeting to evaluate how well the strategies worked and what else might be needed.

The Disinterested Boy

Struggling children often feign disinterest in reading, but I have yet to meet a child who truly doesn't want to read. When children don't try, there are reasons. They can't do it. They're frightened of failure. The lessons are boring. They need help from someone. What they don't need is ongoing punishment and exclusion.

Punishment Is Not the Answer

Incentives work better than punishments. When we punish children and give the impression we see them as bad, they have no place to go. The way forward is to show them they can do better and they will reap rewards for doing better. Ask Johnny's teacher, counselor, or school psychologist how to offer positives and not negatives. Ask about "buddying" programs in which Johnny could partner another child, either as mentor or as protégé. What about self-esteem programs? Can Johnny be part of any summer camps or adventure weekends? Can he be given special responsibilities in class? Good teachers know how to provide children with jobs that can help them feel special.

Real Life: All Kids Want to Read Like the Others

One boy who remains fondly in my memory is Wesley. When I met him, Wesley was a 13-year-old high school student of above-average size and above-average nuisance rating. He was an "in your face" type: big, exuberant, loud, and often disrespectful. Wesley was a recurrent subject of debate and concern in the staff room. He was popularly regarded as arrogant and undisciplined. He was often outside the principal's office.

But in my small remedial group, Wesley, though still irrepressible, was helpful and kind. And he worked hard. Wesley worked harder than the others because he had to. When his classmates grasped a skill, Wesley continued to be perplexed. When other kids were reading chapter books, Wesley stayed with single words. But Wesley persevered.

Every day, when Wesley left my class to go to his mainstream classes, full of his seemingly endless good humor, I knew he would laugh his way through the start of each class but would end up outside the principal's office. Why was he such a problem outside the remedial class? Because he had no hope of succeeding in the regular class, so he learned to keep people laughing instead. He kept attention focused on what he could do, rather than on his weaknesses. Could he learn to read, though, even at the age of 13, and did he want to? Yes. Wesley wanted to read even though his couldn't-care-less exterior masked his real hopes and determination. He worked diligently in the remedial class, and he left school able to read. I smile when I think of Wesley, and feel sure he's making other people smile now too. I'd love one day to meet any children he might have. I'm sure Wesley will have taught them to look deeper than first appearances.

IN SHORT

- Once Johnny starts falling behind, he covers his failure. He may act up or adopt a "couldn't care less" attitude.
- When teachers, parents, and peers have negative expectations of Johnny, he may come to see himself in the same way.
- Johnny really wants to read like his classmates, even if he feigns indifference.
- Blame is never productive; we should focus on solutions, not blame.

CHAPTER 10

Guiding Johnny's Behavior

ENCOURAGING GOOD BEHAVIOR

Boys are more likely than girls to misbehave in school, and this likelihood increases when they have reading problems. So it's important that we help them. We want them to feel good about themselves, to be liked, and to avoid getting into trouble. We want to encourage their best behavior and show them more good ways to behave. But how exactly? By rewarding preferred behavior. With smiles, treats, hugs, praise, and simply by giving our warm attention, we shape Johnny's behavior. We encourage him to repeat the behavior we reward him for; we reinforce the good behavior.

Behavior Management in School

When teachers encourage good behavior with reward systems (stars, points, competitions, and treats) it's called behavior management. Teachers guide and control students by devising lots of ways to recognize and reward good behavior. Done properly, behavior management always makes a difference. But careful planning and maintenance is the key. Some people use charts and incentive schemes haphazardly and find they don't work. This doesn't mean behavior management doesn't work; rather, it means the person using it hasn't been well organized.

Behavior Management Is Consistent

Behavior management gives simple ways to respond to Johnny's behavior. You don't have to worry about different techniques for different situations because reinforcement is a constant technique, similar for every situation.

Behavior Management at Home

If you want to use behavior management techniques at home, go to Johnny's school for help. There will probably be someone (a counselor, psychologist, social worker, resource teacher, special education teacher, or guidance officer) who is versed in behavior-management techniques and can guide you. If not, the district will help or direct you to someone who can help. Your first practical step at home will be to tell everyone in the family what's going on. You might say something like this:

> "Things around here have been noisy and angry lately. I know I shout a lot, and I want to start putting that right. I want us to work out ways of making sure we treat each other better. I want us to get along happily. How do you feel about that?"

Next, decide what you want to achieve and list your wants. Use phrases that say things you actually want, as opposed to things you don't want. For example:

Don't say it this way . . .	. . . say it this way
"I don't want to be yelling all the time."	"I want Johnny to answer me when I talk to him, and to use polite speech to me."
"I don't want to be forever picking up Johnny's things."	"I want Johnny to put his shoes in the closet, and his dirty clothes into the laundry basket."

This now translates into:

Johnny's List

- Answer Mom when she talks, (a simple "mmm" is fine)
- Talk in a polite way.
- Put shoes in closet.
- Put dirty laundry in basket.

Johnny now has manageable goals. Your own list might be:

Mom's List

- Speak in a normal voice.
- Move away from an angry situation.
- Offer alternatives when things go wrong (don't blame).

Rewards

Behavior management is always based on rewards. Smiles, hugs, positive comments, extra TV time, favorite foods, ice cream, play time with friends, excursions, small gifts, money, and clothes are all rewards. Get into the habit of seeing all the good things Johnny does. When Johnny puts his shoes in the closet, acknowledge it. When he talks in a normal voice, acknowledge it. Notice and remark on all the good things. Keep up with comments and smiles always, and give planned rewards, too.

Charts Help Parents Too

Said one dad of his son's rewards chart (in which a rocket went farther toward space for good behavior), "It's more to teach me than to teach Justin. I wouldn't remember to say anything nice or notice the good things if I didn't keep seeing the chart."

Younger Children Love Rewards Charts

Rewards charts are especially good with younger children. But be lavish with rewards. For smaller children, you might give a sticker every time the child does something good, like saying thank you or putting books away. When Johnny has earned 20 stickers, you might let him have an ice cream. After five sets of 20, when Johnny has had five ice creams, he gets a video too. For older children, you might keep a points chart. Remember to work in sets. Johnny gets a small prize for every 10 or 20 points and an additional prize for 50 or 100 points. Set a value on the prizes so they don't get expensive. Some older boys prefer to work only for the one grand prize, but even so, you might give a chocolate bar or a favorite lunch treat after a set of 10, just because you're a great parent!

Don't Take Points Away

If you take points away after giving them, Johnny will think it's not worth being good now because you'll only take points away later. Taking points away kills incentive and shouldn't be done.

Rewards Don't Have to Be Tangible Things

Smiles, appreciative comments, and praise are all effective rewards. You don't have to keep racking your brains for more treats; instead, give some of yourself. Your attention and admiration are precious to Johnny, and will still be precious to him when he's grown up! And don't stop the hugs, either. Whether Johnny is 5 or 15, give him hugs. We all like hugs, even though it's important for teenage boys to pretend they don't. (If Johnny really is a no-hug guy, do the next best thing—whatever he *is* comfortable with.)

A Word of Caution about Threats

Try not to turn rewards into threats. Avoid saying:

"If you shout at me, you won't get a point."

Threats spoil behavior modification. When you threaten Johnny, he's rarely motivated to behave better. Instead, he feels angry and resentful. He may misbehave in defiance or frustration, and then you've backed yourself into a corner because you've no reward to offer.

If you think threats aren't so bad, try putting yourself in Johnny's shoes. Imagine your boss threatens you by saying:

"You won't get your coffee break if you work so slowly."

How do you feel? Are you motivated to try harder, or do you work harder but hate your boss? Do you keep the same pace to get back at your boss? Might you leave the job if the consequences weren't dire?

What if, on the other hand, your boss speaks encouragingly?

"That's a tough job; do you need help?"

or:

"I sympathize with you on that one; you'll be glad when it's done, won't you!"

How do you feel now?

A Word of Caution about Bribes

Try not to use the "carrot and stick" technique either. Don't, for example, say:

"Put your shoes away and you'll get a sticker."

This can lead to Johnny always asking:

"Will I get a reward if I do?"

Or he might decide to tell you:

"I don't want your rewards anyway."

The Way to Avoid Threats and Bribes Is to Rephrase What You Say

If you're tempted to threaten or bribe, which we usually are, rephrase your words into a comment on what you see or what may naturally happen:

> "If you play with the paper, it won't be clean anymore."
> "If you spend time talking, we may be rushed with the other things we have planned."
> "If you don't put your things away, your room will be so untidy. Here, let's do it together."
> "That work is hard; you can be really proud of yourself when you finish it."
> "I'm so pleased to see how you persevere."

These comments are about natural consequences and ordinary observations. We often try to think of rewards and punishments unnecessarily. Our children are happy with our attention and simple comments. If we practice just commenting on what we see Johnny doing, we don't get panicked into immediately trying to bribe or threaten. Children warm to people who are interested in them and talk fondly to them.

Consequences of Misbehavior

Consequences are small punishments for misdemeanors. We must be sure to use consequences sparingly and in small proportions.

Using Consequences Sparingly

Negative consequences are effective if they're used sparingly and in a caring spirit. You can teach Johnny the seriousness of a misdemeanor simply by telling him you're disappointed and trust it won't happen again. You can let Johnny know he's loved and valued, but his behavior is wrong. Consequences need only be small, as long as the serious message is given. A child who behaved dangerously outside might be told you expect better next time and he should spend 30 minutes in quiet indoor play to recover his more responsible attitude.

Consequences should be more symbolic than real with older boys too. Consequences for older boys might be no TV for a weekend or no visits to friends for a week. If you often give harsh punishments, like grounding for a month, you might not get the effect you want. When children are repeatedly and severely punished, they learn subterfuge, resentment, fear, and hatred.

It's All Very Well Saying That Johnny Needs to Be Supported and Rewarded

When Johnny smugly says, "You can't make me," and it's all we can do not to scream, rewards seem to be the last thing we want! Don't despair. Rewards work, but Johnny needs limits and firmness, too. We have lots of bargaining power because, after all, we provide him with everything he has! Move away from heated situations. Get a drink, a snack, or a few breaths of fresh air. Come back to the issue later. State your consequences, and carry them through. And do it knowing that your consequences aren't excessive. Bring things back on track with rewards. You can give a consequence for one thing while still rewarding the many other positive things.

Using Consequences of Small Proportions

Give yourself a short list of progressive consequences. These might be:

10 minutes away from me (you can point out that you feel
angry and 10 minutes to yourself will help)
20 minutes of the same
30 minutes less TV time than usual
A day without TV

The consequences may be different for older boys, but apply
the same principles. Make consequences start with something
small and progress in reasonable, not extreme, measures.

Don't Be Afraid to Enforce Consequences for Noncompliance

Always carry out (predefined) consequences, and do it quickly and
without discussion. If you're sending Johnny to his room, don't
encourage debate or fuss by listening to his complaints or adding
comments. Simply say, "Go to your room for 30 minutes," and
repeat it if necessary. You can calmly say it two or three times,
but don't get into anything more. With small children, you may
need to carry them to their room two or three times before they
learn that you won't be swayed. Keep repeating your command
and putting Johnny in his room, and then start his time (10, 20,
or 30 minutes). Supply him with books or other quiet activities,
but not TV. Johnny may be infuriated the first few times, but it
will get easier. Once the rules are established and he knows what
to expect, outbursts will be fewer and milder. Exclude him until
he "toes the line" again.

Increasing the Severity of Punishments Doesn't Teach a Lesson Any Better

We want to show Johnny not so much that we will punish him as that we are firm and definitely in control.

Sometimes We Can Soften the Consequences

When Johnny is used to your methods, it's sometimes OK to remind him of all the good things you do at the same time as you enforce a consequence. For instance, you can often squash Johnny's rising anger by saying something like, "Go to your room for 30 minutes because I don't expect to be yelled at. When you come out, there are cookies for you to have while you do your home-work, and later we'll watch the rest of the video." (This doesn't sound so likely to arouse wrath, does it?) Johnny will probably go quietly, especially if he's used to this sort of routine. If he doesn't, restart the timer: "I will start your time when you're in your room."

Some Extra Tips for Using Consequences

- Avoid yelling. Instead, move away, put on soothing music, have a snack or drink.
- Don't use lengthy punishments or delay the onset of a punishment.
- Don't go for a big punishment because you're momen-tarily enraged. It's all too easy for us to start a war with our child.
- Give out the first punishment, and when 10 minutes is up, give Johnny a chance to atone. (Remember, a broken plate will seem far less serious 10 minutes later.)
- In bad times, go straight to your list of moderately escalating consequences.
- Remember that your ultimate goal is more peace and harmony at home.
- Don't be swayed by hard-liners who try to tell you Johnny needs bigger punishments "he won't forget in a hurry." Big, bad punishments don't teach better lessons and can backfire. Johnny grows up resentful, and we wonder why he doesn't visit us often.

If Consequences Bother You

If consequences bother you, you can do without them. Anthony Wolf, psychologist and author, describes a way of doing without punishments altogether. Be firm in your decisions, says Wolf, but simply say no (in as short a way as you can) and don't get into any further discussion or fussing. Kids want your attention (and to go on fussing!), so deprive them of it to convey your displeasure. Wolf says by doing this, we teach our kids to do the right thing because they have a conscience, not because they want to avoid punishment.

WHAT IF BEHAVIOR MANAGEMENT DOESN'T WORK?

When you use behavior management techniques, but still get into angry incidents, it doesn't mean all is lost. Go straight back to your list of goals and forgive yourself for lapses. In the big picture, you'll be making progress. Talk to Johnny about the list you have. Tell him that you know, just as he does, that things have been unorganized and angry. Ask him if he can tell you the things that lead to arguments. Try to get him to give you a list or help you write one. Ask him, "What would you say are our worse difficulties? What gets me shouting?" If you get caught up in accusations, turn them into relevant points on your list. For example, suppose Johnny says:

> "You're always yelling at me, whatever I do; you're always so moody. I hate your tantrums."

Don't retaliate. He's just saying how he feels. Remember you're going to attend to the problem situation, not the problem boy. You might say:

> "Yes, I get mad, and I'm going to work on that. Let's be specific and get something written down. I'm going to write about talking in a normal voice. Do you think we could both have a go at that?"

The "4 to 1 Rule"

A very good school psychologist once told me the "4 to 1 Rule." We must give children enough positives that they outnumber the negatives by *at least* 4 to 1. Then children will want to be good so they don't miss out on all the good things.

Behavior Management Has a "Use By" Date

Behavior management systems often have a limited life. When you find the system becoming less effective, don't worry; this is normal. Take a break from the scheme and then set up a new one. Your goals usually change anyway. Johnny may no longer need to focus on manners; maybe doing homework is more of a concern now. Talk it over with him.

Talk Is All-Important

What we say to Johnny is as important as the way we act with him. Few of us are always positive; we're only human. But we go on trying. We know it will always be important for us to talk to our children in positive ways, and we see examples of this all around us. Some of the "good talk" rules are:

Instead of Being Vague or Saying How Bad Johnny Has Been	Describe What Needs to Be Done
You always go wandering off.	You must stay close by me in here.
You've left these pens out again; why do you always do it?	The pens must be put away.
Every time I come to use this table, you've left it in a mess; you're so untidy!	I expect you to wipe the table down, please.
You never let me talk; you're always interrupting. Can't you see I'm busy? Go away!	You must play here for 10 minutes, so I can talk to my friends.

Instead of Blaming, Complaining, or Using "I Don't Want" Statements	Use "I Feel" or "I Want" Statements
You're always yelling. Why can't you behave like a normal boy?	I feel really cross when you yell.
Isn't it about time you got your book instead of messing around all night?	I want you to get your book, please.
I'm sick of you always being on that computer; you never do anything else!	I want you to tidy up in 5 minutes, please.
You never think of helping me, do you?	I want you to help me clean up, please.
I'm not here just to be yelled at!	I want you to use a normal voice, please.

Instead of Blaming, Complaining, or Using "I Don't Want" Statements	Use "I Feel" or "I Want" Statements
Your pens are all over the floor again. I've told you a million times about these stupid pens. Shall I throw them all out? Are they so unimportant to you?	I want you to pick up your pens, please.

Instead of Using Threats or Insults	Use "We" Statements
You always talk too loudly. Why can't you talk like other people?	We use a quiet voice in here.
If you don't clean it up, it goes in the trash!	We need to clean up now.
Pick it up or throw it out!	We can pick these up together, can't we?
Your books are always on the floor. How many times must I tell you?	I'll help you with the books; we can work together.
Get a move on, stop dawdling!	We must move quickly or we'll be late.
Get moving now. You sit around wasting time instead of helping!	We have to leave in 5 more minutes.
You moan all the time; you're so miserable and ungrateful, Mr. Moan-A-Lot.	We could leave this and go out.
You're always so selfish.	We need to share.
You've left your stuff right in the path again. That's it, no TV!	We must put this box somewhere safe.

Instead of Attending to the Problem	Attend to the Solution
You're always fighting. Can't you share anything? Go to your room!	You need to ask your sister if you want to borrow her pen.
Stop pulling that book. You're both like a pair of wild animals!	You need to take turns if you want the same thing.
Your room is a pigsty. Why are you so selfish? I do everything around here!	The clothes must be put away before TV starts.
Where's your homework? How come you think you can just sit around watching TV?	Homework must be finished before the TV goes on.
Why is that noise on? I can't even talk on the phone for 1 minute. Get out of here!	Please ask me before you put the music on.
Give me those cookies. You don't deserve to have cookies when you fight like dogs over the stupid cookies. Can't you share anything?	Cookies must be shared.
I told you not to touch that. What's wrong with you, are you deaf?	That's fragile, so I want you not to touch it.
Look at this mess. How can you do this again after I've told you? Look how much work you've made for me. Get out of my sight!	Food must never go into the bedroom.
You're a bully. Shall I hit you so you can see how it feels?	We can't hit each other; people get hurt.
Stop snatching! Why are you so rude?	We ask politely for the things we want.

But Don't Forget to Listen!

The older our children get, the less they want us "bothering" them! They start off wanting us to listen to their every word and watch their every demonstration, but it doesn't seem long before they're ignoring us. It's hard to squeeze conversation from our child, and boys are often less talkative than girls. But we can make things better by being a good listener. Start off early, when Johnny is at the age where he seeks you out. Listen without interruption; don't judge. Get as much out of him as you can by being attentive, by paraphrasing, and by encouraging him to say more.

Being Attentive

This is all about eye contact and brief comments. Make sure you look at Johnny when he's talking (even if it's only a quick look now and then because you're busy with something) and respond to his comments, but briefly! "Mmm" and "oh" are fine as long as the general message is that you're listening. You can do other things while you're listening, and can even cruise through interruptions, as long as you keep the "I'm listening" mood going and, in the case of interruptions, get back to what he was saying. Don't offer any more though, unless he asks. Above all else, he wants you to listen. He usually doesn't want you to solve his problems, offer advice, or ask for more. You're just his sounding board, and should get used to it! He also wants to keep conversation short. Older boys in particular are minimalists with conversation (it's excruciating for them if Mom talks too much) and very self-interested (in case you hadn't noticed).

Paraphrasing

Paraphrasing is when you feed Johnny's comments back to him in an abridged form. You repeat key parts of his conversation to encourage him to say more. Like this:

"I didn't hear the teacher speak to me, and I turned around to tell Joe something. She went crazy. She started yelling at me and telling the whole class how bad I am."

"You didn't hear her?"

"No, but she thought I was being smart."

"She misunderstood."

"She sure did."

You have kept the conversation going, and you're eliciting more.

This is all you need to do. The tricky part is *not* saying the things you're bursting to say:

"You did *what*?"

"*Why* weren't you listening?"

"*Why* were you trying to talk to Joe when you should've been listening?"

This is, of course, what we want to say, but if we say it, Johnny ends the conversation, reminds himself not to tell us anything again, and doesn't take any notice of what we said anyway!

Encouraging Johnny to Say More

Do this with "must've" statements.

"That must've made you feel bad."

"That must've been hard."

"That must've been embarrassing."

"That must've frustrated you."

Commenting on how things must've felt or seemed to Johnny encourages him to elaborate. You're letting him know you have empathy. He will trust you and want to confide in you if he feels you understand him.

Listening to Johnny is one of the best things we will ever do. Later, when we most want him to trust us, he will. In his teenage years and beyond, he may pay us the ultimate tribute of spending time with us, chatting and confiding.

When Is Advice Not Advice?

It's not advice when Johnny doesn't hear it, let alone follow it! Give advice sparingly or when Johnny asks for it. When we smother Johnny with our advice, he simply switches off.

WAYS WE CAN CHANGE OUR OWN BEHAVIOR

When we're experts in positive ways of managing, talking, and listening to our kids, we're still not done! Now we have to look at our own behavior. Have we let some things slide?

Ways we can change our own behavior include:

- Allowing Johnny to lead a child's lifestyle (do without fancy restaurants, late nights, or long drives).
- Being around as much as we can and committing our leisure time to Johnny.
- Learning to just be with him, without organized activities.
- Avoiding excessive telephone conversations or other distractions.
- Seeing problem behaviors and not a problem child.
- Understanding that bad behavior can result from the humiliation Johnny feels when he can't read.
- Understanding that when Johnny misbehaves, he's suffering, even though he appears to be inflicting the suffering.
- Learning to walk away from heated situations, hopefully just before they become heated. Go back to the situation when you're calm. You'll keep your own nerves steady and encourage Johnny not to fly off the handle too.

Real Life: Spotting the Good Things Our Children Do

When 8-year-old Jessie got up, she was full of bad temper. Tom, her younger brother, was a hapless target.

"Get out of my way, you brat. I need to get into that closet, and you're purposely going too slow!"

She threw her clothes across the floor and pronounced that she wasn't going to school; she hated school, all they ever did was work, work, work. Also, she was fat and all her clothes made her look even fatter. Her friends would walk away from her. Her sock tickled. Composed and ever helpful, her mom yelled:

"Why do you always have to be in such a foul mood in the mornings? I'm sick of you always being so horrible. There are no more socks, so you'll have to wear these. Stop yelling! I'm going in 10 minutes, and you're coming, whatever state you're in, so you'd better get your clothes on. I'll drag you out if I have to!"

Not one to miss an opportunity, Tom joined in the general medley:

"I'm not going to school either. This toothbrush is too hard; I'm not going to use it."

At this stage, Mom pulled Tom from the bathroom so roughly that he cried. In her head she planned to stop TV for the rest of the week.

Mornings like this tell mortal moms that it's probably essential to have parenting "survival" lists. We go blank, and suddenly find ourselves doing all the wrong things. We've read the books, but can't stop to review them in the middle of our crises. A single phrase might help—perhaps "praise achievements." Armed with the mental inscription "praise achievements," Mom might've seen what Jessie had actually achieved. Despite her moaning, Jessie had accomplished two good things: She had made her bed and eaten breakfast. Mom would surely have felt better if she had praised the (albeit few) good things Jessie had done. She might have elevated the morning's tone. She might have moved the children on, instead of stopping to admonish and blame them. She might have mentally sailed above the furor and quickly left it behind her. But instead, her pulse raced, the children became worse, and for the rest of the morning she seethed and planned retribution. By the afternoon she was racked with guilt over her own bad behavior and terrible feelings.

PARENTS SURVIVAL LIST: SAMPLE

How to Behave

- Give short, clear instructions.
- Reward all good behaviors.
- Model polite ways.
- Move away from angry situations; give yourself a time-out.
- At fractious times, move yourself and your children quickly on to other things.
- Find solutions; avoid blame.
- Separate warring children to stop the war continuing.

How to Talk

- Be solution-oriented.
- Talk in terms of the act, incident, or difficulty, rather than in terms of the offender or his personal deficiencies.
- Talk politely yourself.
- Praise all achievements.
- Find solutions; avoid blame.

(continued on next page)

- Encourage children to talk in normal voices and ask for what they want (no yelling, demanding, or threatening).
- Teach children to take turns.
- Encourage children to find their own solutions.

How to Listen
- Paraphrase and reflect back what Johnny said.
- Avoid comment unless Johnny asks for it.
- Don't interrupt.
- Invite Johnny to tell you more.
- Comment on how he must have felt or how the situation must've seemed to him.
- Don't judge or solve problems. (When we have problems, we want to be heard and understood. We seldom want others to solve our problem for us.)

THE GREAT CHECKLIST

We can't talk of guiding Johnny's behavior without including checklists. It's almost certain Johnny won't be naturally blessed with good work habits or organizational skills, so he needs checklists to help him. Provide paper and pen, and your time, so he can compile simple lists. Sit with him and make suggestions in a sensitive way, just as you might with another adult. Become another helpful person, not the boss, and certainly not the critic. Ask Johnny what he needs to do, help him break his tasks down into steps. If writing is tedious for him, offer to be his secretary.

You might end up with something like this:

Sunday Night
Check inside pencil case for pencils, pens, erasers, ruler (replace or sharpen if needed).

Pack schoolbag: lunch money, library book, bus pass, pencil case.
Lay out clothes, including shoes.
Check that keys are hanging on hook.

Monday Night

Do spelling words.
Check inside pencil case for pencils, pens, erasers, ruler (replace or sharpen if needed).
Pack schoolbag: lunch money, bus pass, pencil case, spelling words.
Lay out clothes, including shoes.
Check that keys are hanging on hook.

Always Be Solution-Oriented

Allow time to go through the checklist, if possible at the same time each night, to establish a routine. If your routine is disturbed, help Johnny complete his tasks. Do this even if Johnny has been responsible for the disturbance, for example, by staying out later than he should have. Avoid blaming, and instead solve the immediate problem. If he has lost his pen, hand him another; if he hasn't brought home his homework, suggest he phone a friend to get it as best he can; if his homework is just too hard, do it with him and write a note to the teacher, or leave it and write an explanatory note to the teacher. If he broke your rules, give a reasonable consequence or find a way he can atone. Remember that none of us wants to feel bad about ourselves and when things go wrong, we need support and solutions or alternatives. When Mom is solution-oriented, Johnny feels appreciative. His feelings toward Mom are warm, even though he may not be demonstrative. If Mom blames and scolds, Johnny has entirely different feelings toward her and the problem at hand.

> ### *Without Our Help, It's Unlikely That Johnny Will Be Able to Organize the Paperwork That Comes from School*
>
> Most days Johnny gets a sizable wad of things to be filed, discarded, signed and immediately returned, or signed and returned later. It's hard enough for parents to keep track, and certainly too much for Johnny to do by himself.

Problem Solving

One helpful way to encourage Johnny to organize his tasks and solve problems for himself is to teach him "the three Ps" strategy:

- Problem
- Possibilities
- Practice

Problem

First define the problem. What is it exactly, and why is it happening? Let's say that Johnny can't get his homework handed in at school. When he thinks about why this happens, he thinks it's because the homework is too hard.

Possibilities

Now Johnny thinks of possible solutions to the problem:

- Ask Mom to do the homework with me.
- Get a tutor.
- Join a homework club.
- Get Mom to talk to the teacher.

Practice

Johnny chooses one or two of the possible solutions and tries them straightaway.

If Johnny uses this framework, it may become a regular habit in times of need. Be sure to help him be at the helm of this ship; he needs to adopt his own strategies and become more able to deal with problems himself. The hands-off approach is again the best way to help. Children are nearly always able to do their own problem solving and usually don't want our interference. What they want us to do is listen, empathize, and help them gather their thoughts.

IN SHORT

- Effective parents look for solutions (and avoid blaming). Ditto for teachers.
- Parenting and teaching are learned skills. Watching good teachers and parents, reading books, and attending parenting courses are all good ways to learn.
- Checklists help us to be more organized and in control.
- One way to solve problems is to focus on the three Ps: problem, possibilities, and practice.
- Rewards and focusing on positive aspects of Johnny's behavior increase the likelihood that good behavior will be repeated.
- Threats and bribes damage rewards systems.
- Punishments must be given only occasionally and with restraint.

Extras

Top 10 Most Frequently Asked Questions

1. *How Do I Know If Johnny Has a Reading Problem?*
From Johnny's friends we get an idea of how other kids read. If we're concerned, chances are Johnny *is* on the road to having reading problems. Can he read simple phonically regular words? Does he know the 220 sight words by sight? Pinpoint the areas he is weak in and give him practical help.

2. *When Do Children Start to Read?*
Most children start to read between the ages of 5 and 7.

3. *Should I Get My Son Tested?*
If Johnny seems to be a very long way behind, you can ask the school to test him for a learning disability. Put your request in writing. However, if you're fairly sure Johnny won't qualify as having a learning disability, even though he's struggling, think about why you would need testing. Be sure that test results will be useful to you before getting tests done, and don't delay getting Johnny practical instruction in phonics.

4. *Should I Give Johnny Time to Be Developmentally Ready?*
Between the ages of 5 and 7, Johnny should start to read. If he doesn't, act quickly. Have Johnny's teacher give you work to do with him at home. Ask about extra help in school. If you pay for private tutoring, get a tutor you feel confident in and consider

your money well spent. Developmental readiness is a good concept, but not for reading problems. Age 5 to 7 is crucial, and waiting doesn't pay off.

5. *What Do* Dyslexia *and* Learning Disability *Really Mean?*

In ordinary language, these terms describe unexpected and pronounced problems with reading and writing. But even though they're used widely, they have to be confirmed by school district tests or approved private tests to count in school and earn Johnny special education services. As a rough rule of thumb, Johnny may qualify at school as having a learning disability (or dyslexia, which is one type of learning disability) if he's performing about 2 years below his potential.

6. *How Can I Help at Home?*

The backbone of reading is phonics. Get some fun workbooks and CD-ROMs and use them frequently. Establish regular times to work with Johnny, and get guidance from his teacher. Your other best tool for helping Johnny read is the 220 sight words. See that Johnny has instant recognition of these words.

7. *Are There Any Good CD-ROMs I Can Use?*

Use educational CD-ROMs based on phonics. As long as Johnny enjoys the books and CD-ROMs you use, they're probably good. The thing to watch out for is that Johnny can't blindly memorize the correct responses. He will certainly learn to memorize, but make sure it's good memorizing. If he has learned *pin* by sight, that's good, but if he's just giving the answer in the top left corner, that's not good. Bear in mind too that your presence and guidance will improve Johnny's progress enormously. Don't do the work for him, but *do* be there at the computer with him to give your interest and support.

8. *Should I Get a Tutor?*

There are lots of good reasons to get a tutor—you're too close to the problem, you don't feel confident about teaching, you want to give the job to a professional. Get tutoring at school if it's offered, and get private tutoring if you can afford it. Get a tutor who's organized and runs a structured program based on phonics. Be sure she can show you results.

9. *Which Is Better, a Tutor or a Learning Center?*

Both of these options are good as long as Johnny likes and respects the tutor and the tutor runs a professional program. Her program must be structured, sequential, and results-based. You want Johnny to follow progressive steps and show improvement.

10. *What about Older Children?*

There's no doubt that older children have to work harder than the 5- to 7-year-olds. But that doesn't mean an older boy can't make great progress. With lots of support and a structured program, Johnny will move forward. Be sure to reward him for his efforts and have him tutored frequently. A good plan is for Johnny to be tutored two or three times a week and have tutoring homework too. If you can't afford such frequent tutoring, you can have Johnny see the tutor once a week, but be sure to get lots of good homework.

Top 10 Quickest and Best Tips

1. Dictation

Dictation is when we read aloud to Johnny and he writes it down. That's all. That's all it takes to help Johnny enormously. Try a short dictation every night for a month. Choose a paragraph with only two or three tricky words, and repeat it twice before choosing a new one. Johnny will build speed, accuracy, and confidence.

2. Proofreading

Help Johnny write in short, clear sentences and proofread. When Johnny reads his work aloud, does it make sense? Are the simple words spelled correctly? Are there enough periods? Are the periods in the right places? Don't nag Johnny to death because you see a million mistakes, but encourage him to correct the mistakes he can see. If he can't see an error, just give him the correction and practice it. (Trying to squeeze a correct answer from him will frustrate you both.)

3. Punctuation

Check that Johnny understands what periods and commas mean. A little teaching of punctuation can go a long way.

4. Visual Discrimination

When Johnny learns words by sight, he's using visual discrimination. He's noticing the shape of letters and words. You can help him sharpen this skill by getting out his puzzle books. Spot the difference, make pairs, and find the hidden object will all improve Johnny's ability to visually discriminate. Jotting words down on paper is the other way to hone Johnny's visual skills. Teach Johnny to write down spelling guesses and choose the word that looks best ("practice spelling"). Apart from sounding out, this is the number one way we get better at spelling.

5. Look, Say, Cover, Write, Check

This is the formula for learning a word by sight. If a word can't be sounded out, have Johnny *look* at it and *say* it aloud, then *cover* it over and *write* it from memory. Last of all, *check* for correct spelling. Do this several times for a word or group of words, but limit a group of words to 10 at most. Highlight any distinctive features of a word (e.g., two letters that are the same or a familiar group of letters, like *ight*). Sound out wherever you can.

6. Handwriting

When Johnny complains about handwriting, check his technique and persevere. Fluid handwriting does more than make Johnny's writing neat. If Johnny writes smoothly and quickly, he can devote more thought to spelling. His handwriting won't use up the concentration he needs for his spelling.

7. Reading "Around" a Book

To make a book easier for Johnny to read, prepare him for what's inside the pages. Talk about the illustrations and what the plot might be. Identify tricky words. Read the book to him the first time around if he wants you to. Have Johnny read and reread the book so he feels confident and fluent.

8. Computers
Buy educational computer games and do deals with Johnny if you need to. For example, every 30 minutes on the phonics game earns Johnny 10 minutes free choice. But don't forget that Johnny will learn *much* more from educational CDs if you're involved. Sit with him. Guide him. Praise his successes.

9. Note Taking
When Johnny can't write as quickly as his peers, note taking is a great help. Teach Johnny to write only key words. Ask the teacher to underline the key words when she writes instructions on the board. If Johnny copies those words, they will jog his memory to remember the rest of the instructions.

10. Car Games
Johnny needs to hear word parts so he can write them down. You can help him with this "phonemic awareness" by playing simple games. Try these:

- How many words can you think of that end in *ing*? start with *ch*? have three syllables?
- How many girl's names can you think of that start with *M, T, S* . . . ?
- Think of a boy's name for each letter of the alphabet, e.g., Andrew, Bob, Colin.
- Sing a song with a girl's name in it.
- See what new games *you* can think of!

Jargon Made Easy

Jargon	What It Really Means
Auditory discrimination and visual discrimination	Auditory discrimination is the ability to hear differences in words and word parts. Visual discrimination is the ability to see those differences.
Behavior management	Years ago the psychologists Skinner and Pavlov told us how they made rats and dogs behave in ways they had "conditioned." They had rewarded the behaviors they wanted from the animals, and consequently the animals did more of those behaviors. (They also showed that punishments weren't nearly as effective as rewards in eliciting desired behavior.) Today's behavior management uses the same principles. We encourage kids to behave well by rewarding the good behaviors we want.
Developmental readiness	Maturity, or how ready Johnny is in terms of his own development. This is largely inaccessible to anyone else. Whether he is or isn't mature enough is largely independent of what you do (assuming normal environmental stimulation).
Diagnostic assessment	*Diagnostic* means a course of treatment will be recommended. *Assessment* means testing and analyzing results.

Jargon	What It Really Means
Digraph, diphthong, phonogram, phoneme, blend	Fancy terms for sounds or parts within words. A digraph is two letters that together make one new sound, like *ch* and *sh*; a diphthong is two vowels that together make one sound, like *ea* and *ee*; phonograms and phonemes are parts or units of sound in a word (i.e., *g-o*, *sh-e*). A blend is two or three letters that combine to make a blended sound, like *bl* and *str*.
Dyslexia	Johnny may be called dyslexic if he is unexpectedly and enduringly unable to read.
Individual Education Plan (IEP)	A program for an individual child with disabilities. The IEP is a working document written and reviewed regularly by a team, usually called the Child Study Team.
Individuals with Disabilities Education Act (IDEA)	This act specifies how special education must be provided for children with disabilities.
Learning differences; reading difficulties; specific learning difficulties; special needs	Terms used when Johnny struggles but has not been formally diagnosed with a specific learning disability. Just to confuse us, they may be used when he has been formally diagnosed with a specific learning disability too.
Sight words, most frequent words, most common words, high-frequency words	Words that should be learned to a level of instant recognition because they constitute about 70 percent of all writing.

Jargon	What It Really Means
Phonemic awareness, phonological awareness, phonics, graphophonics, phonographics	Phonemic or phonological awareness is the ability to hear that words are made of sounds. It's taught as a very first skill, before introducing letters. Phonics is showing that letters and letter groups represent those sounds; graphophonics and phonographics mean focusing on the visual shapes of letters and letter groups while you're teaching sounds.
Program	A plan of work. A program may be for general use, as when a teacher uses a program for the entire class, or it may be individually tailored to meet Johnny's specific needs, as in the case of programs designed by private consultants.
	Some of the better-known commercial reading programs include Reading Recovery; "Distar" and "Corrective Reading" (both produced by SRA); Lindamood-Bell (LIPS); PACE/Master the Code; Orton-Gillingham Phonics; Chapter 1 Reading; Project Read; Slingerland; Spalding; and Wilson Language Training.
Section 504 of the Rehabilitation Act of 1973	If Johnny doesn't qualify as having a learning disability, this act may help you.
Self-fulfilling prophecy	Researchers use this expression to describe how a teacher can unconsciously influence students' behavior. The students live up (or down) to the teacher's expectations.

Jargon	What It Really Means
Resource teacher (sometimes called support teacher)	The person who supports children who have disabilities. She provides support in all or any of these ways: • Helping teachers modify work • Helping students in their regular class or a special class • Withdrawing students from class for special instruction
Specific Learning Disability	Federal law identifies educational disabilities. Among them is Specific Learning Disability (SLD), and dyslexia is a subset of this.

Web Sites/Contacts

FAVORITES

www.hellofriend.org
Site of the Ennis William Cosby Foundation. Easy to read and use, with moving personal stories.

www.ldonline.com
Site of the Coordinated Campaign for Learning Disabilities (CCLD). Clear text; masses of topics. Gives the option of basic or in-depth information.

www.ldpride.net
(telephone: 250-478-4554)
A friendly site. Easy text and navigation; lots of information; a chat room and bulletin board.

www.literacytrust.org.uk
A UK site, friendly, easy to use, and packed with information

www.nichcy.org
(telephone: 800-695-0285)
Site of the National Information Center for Children and Youth with Disabilities (NICHCY). Although this site doesn't look immediately inviting, it has loads of information, clear and simple text, personal stories, and free information kits and publications.

www.ld.org
(telephone: general info, 888-575-7373;
detailed info, 212-545-7510)
Site of the National Center for Learning Disabilities (NCLD). This site looks too busy at first, but the text is easy to read and the information is straightforward and abundant. The fast facts are very interesting

www.readingpains.com
What a great site! (This is my own site, it's friendly and easy to navigate and has articles, parents' stories, and information about my books and talks.)

www.schwablearning.org
(telephone: 650-655-2410)
Site of the Schwab Foundation for Learning. Easy to read and follow, with loads of information.

OTHER USEFUL SITES

www.aetonline.org
(telephone: 818-843-1183)
Association of Educational Therapists (AET)

www.educate.com
(telephone: 800-310-0278)
Sylvan Learning Center

www.educationalconsulting.org
(telephone: 800-808-IECA)
Independent Educational Consultants Association (IECA)

www.escore.com
(telephone: 800-49-SCORE)
Score Educational Centers

www.interdys.org
(telephone: general information, 800-222-3123;
detailed information, 410-296-0232)
International Dyslexia Association

www.kumon.com
(telephone: 800-ABC-MATH)
Kumon Math and Reading Centers

www.ldanatl.org
(telephone: 888-300-6710 or 412-341-1515)
Learning Disabilities Association of America (LDA)

www.MHteachers.com
(telephone: 800-843-8855 or 888-772-4543)
McGraw-Hill site. Click on the Frank Schaffer icon (a cheery man's face inside a circle, at the top of a column of icons on the right) to see Frank Schaffer products. Click on Language Arts to get to phonics books.

www.nces.ed.gov
(telephone: 202-502-7300)
National Center for Educational Statistics

www.nrrf.org
National Right to Read Foundation

www.pave-eye.com
(telephone: 619-287-0081 or 800-PAVE-988)
Parents Active for Vision Education (PAVE)

www.professionaltutors.com
(telephone: 800-TEACHUS)
Professional Tutors of America Inc.

www.zoo-phonics.com
(telephone: 209-962-5030)
Zoo-phonics materials that help children learn letter sounds.

Best Resources

These have been chosen after years of hands-on experience and hundreds of hours spent in school stores!

PHONICS WORKBOOKS FOR KIDS

When You Teach Johnny Be Actively Involved to Get the Most Benefit

If you leave Johnny to work alone, he won't learn anywhere near as much as when you're involved.

Help Your Child Learn Series

This series has these two titles:

Phonics Vowels, ISBN 0867340045
Phonics Consonant, ISBN 0867340037

Published by Frank Schaffer (a division of McGraw-Hill). For absolute beginners, these books are ultra-simple, dealing only in pictures and single words (*cat, box, leg*). Cut them up once you're done with them and play with the pictures and words (match them or write the word that goes with the picture). Available in school supplies stores or online.*

---

*www.MHteachers.com. Click the top icon on the right (the Frank Schaffer icon, a man's smiling face in a circle). From there, click on Language Arts, then on Phonics.

Homework Helpers Series

This series has these two titles:

Phonics Grade K, ISBN 0768206979
Phonics Grade 1, ISBN 0768207037

Published by Frank Schaffer (a division of McGraw-Hill). These books are another beginners' product, and they're inexpensive and fun. You'll need to pre-teach the occasional sight word like *the* and *was.* Available in school supplies stores or online.*

Zoo-phonics

This is not a book, but a parent kit of cards, instructions, video, CD-ROM, and a bit more. Younger kids love the each-letter-of-the-alphabet-is-an-animal theme. The program is very hands-on, but get guidance from a teacher or resource teacher who uses this program if you can. Allow yourself a few hours to read about the techniques and practice them beforehand (guidebook included). Available from www.zoo-phonics.com.

Explode the Code

Book 1, ISBN 0838814603

Published by Educators Publishing Service; authors Nancy Hall and Rena Price. There are 17 books in this series. The first 3 are prereading books, *Get Ready* (A), *Get Set* (B) and *Go* (C). After this, there are numbered books going from 1 to 8 (the first is listed here), with some half numbers (e.g., $1\frac{1}{2}$) in case Johnny needs more practice. These are phonically regulated, easy-to-use books for any age. Available online at www.epsbooks.com.

Reading Freedom

Reading Freedom 1, ISBN 1740200683
Reading Freedom 2, ISBN 1740200691

Published by Pascal Press; author Hunter Calder. These books are an Australian product, but they're easy to buy online. They're phonically regulated and simple to use, and have an appealing look for older kids. Book 1 gives a list of 240 basic sight vocabulary words and teaches short vowel words and consonant blends in structured lessons that all follow the same format. Have Johnny highlight word families in different colors from the lists given. (By the way, *thong* in Australia means *flip-flop*, not a type of underwear!) Available from www.pascal press.com.au.

Building Spelling Skills

Grade 2, ISBN 155799840X

Published by Evan-Moor. This set of six workbooks (grades 1 to 6) is good for children who are intimidated by seeing too much writing. The units are attractively laid out, with dictation and proofreading activities included. Available online at www.evan-moor.com, by telephone at 800-777-4362, or by fax at 800-777-4332.

With Any Workbook, Always Use Phonically Regulated Reading Books Too

Rhyming and predictable books, and books Johnny writes himself, are nice, but when Johnny reads these, he knows he's doing more remembering than sounding out. Kids want to sound out to feel they're really reading all by themselves. Look under "Kids' Reading Books" for recommendations.

KIDS' READING BOOKS

Don't Forget to Prepare Johnny for Reading

Teach Johnny any unknown words (usually these are sight words) before he tries to read.

Read the book to him first if he wants.
Read it with him if he wants.
Have him read it several times to get fluency and confidence.

Beginners

Bob Books

Published by Scholastic. Small books in a box, 12 books per boxed set. There are three levels, A, B, and C, and more than one set per level. Available in most bookstores.

Primary Phonics

Published by Educators Publishing Service. This is a series of phonetically controlled reading books; 5 sets with 10 books per set. There are workbooks too. You can view and buy these online at www.epsbooks.com. Also available by phone: 800-435-7728 or 617-547-6706.

The Wright Skills

Published by The Wright Group. Lots of books, phonetically graded, with new sight words written on the inside back cover so you can prepare Johnny before reading. Available at www.wright group.com (click on Literacy, ABC's and Assessment, then The Wright Skills).

Level A: short vowels only, student books, 19 books;
ISBN 032206473
Level B: long vowels only, student books, 6 books;
ISBN 0322019346
Level C: 16 books; ISBN 0322007348

Fitzroy Readers

Distributed by Fitzroy Programs. These books are an Australian product, but they're easy to buy online. They come in boxes of 10 and are phonetically controlled, with new sight words listed on the cover. Available from www.fitzprog.com.au.

A Bit Harder

Hop on Pop, Cat in the Hat, Green Eggs and Ham,
Put Me in the Zoo

Published by Random House. These are some of the easiest books of the Dr. Seuss series. Available in most bookstores.

Hardest

Little Bill books for beginning readers, published by Scholastic. Use these after Johnny has mastered the previous books in this list (or books of similar difficulty). Great multicultural style. Available in most bookstores.

What Next?

When Johnny is able to read simple books, he can use book sets. Libraries have these, but check individual books for maturity level, as there are some babyish styles. These are some of the common sets or series:

I Can Read
Step Into Reading
Puffin Easy To Read
All Aboard Reading

Save Money by Using Your Public Library

You'll find most of these books at your local library. If your branch doesn't have an item, it will order it for you.

CD-ROMS

Reader Rabbit series (which progresses to the ClueFinders series)
Jump Start series

Remember to Be Involved When Johnny Uses CD-ROMs

He learns most when you guide and praise him.

COMMERCIAL GAMES

Card games like *Old Maid*
Ants in the Pants (flicking ants into a bucket shaped like pants; remove the figure from the bucket to make it easier)
Chutes and Ladders
Darts with rubber tips and dartboard to match

These Activities Are Great for Punctuating Your Teaching

For example, you can spend 20 minutes on worksheets, then 5 to10 minutes on play. Be sure you play with Johnny rather than leaving him to play alone.

FLASH CARDS

Letter Blocks (choose the lowercase version) by Creative Teaching Press. This is an excellent product because you get plenty of letters plus a few sight words and the words *in, at,* and *an* to make word families from. Available in school supplies stores or online at www.creativeteaching.com.

Easy Vowels box set by Frank Schaffer.* Includes three-letter, short-vowel words you can start with and long-vowel words to use later.

Easy Blends and Digraphs box set by Frank Schaffer.* Use after three-letter words. Do the blends first and the long vowels later.

Self Check series by Frank Schaffer.* This series lets Johnny use a special stencil to check his own work.

Beginning to Read Phonics: Fishing for Silent "e" Words by Judy/Instructo.* The Judy/Instructo cards give a game, and you can play "wacky cards," too (see Chapter 7), as the set includes a few wild cards.

Beginning to Read Phonics: Word Family Fun, Long Vowels by Judy/Instructo.*

OTHER GREAT RESOURCES YOU'LL FIND IN A SCHOOL SUPPLIES STORE

Phonics games. If you play with Johnny frequently, he'll hardly notice he's learning, and you'll have great fun, too.

---

*Frank Schaffer and Judy/Instructo are divisions of McGraw-Hill. These products are available in school supplies stores or online at www.MHteachers.com. For Frank Schaffer products, click the top Frank Schaffer icon on the right (a man's smiling face in a circle), then Language Arts, then Phonics. For Judy/Instructo products, click the Judy/Instructo icon on the right, then Language Arts, then Language Arts (Misc).

Posters. You'll find inexpensive alphabet posters and posters with long vowels, short vowels, beginning blends, ending blends, and high-frequency words. A great investment!

Alphabet stencils. A good, low-effort way to reinforce the letters.

Whiteboards; blackboards; magnetic boards and letters. Low effort, high return.

Letter tiles. Kids will play with these if you play, too.

Notes and References

IMPORTANT RESEARCH

The statements made in this book are supported by educational studies. The most recent extensive study is *Teaching Children to Read*. This study was commissioned by Congress in 1997, with findings released in 2002. A panel of 14 experts, led by the director of the National Institute of Child Health and Human Development (NICHD), examined all the good research and put their findings in the *Teaching Children to Read* report. Dr. Reid Lyon of the NICHD gave statements about *Teaching Children to Read* (and other reports) to media and government groups. He made these points:

Age

With intensive reading instruction, 95 percent of struggling children aged 9 or below can attain average reading levels.

When we help children who are older than 9, we have to be especially organized and vigilant. Only 25 percent of struggling children in this age group catch up.

It's much more time-consuming to teach older children and adults to read than it is to teach 5- or 6-year-olds. You can improve the skills of a struggling kindergartner or first grader four times more quickly than you can a struggling fourth grader.

Without systematic, focused, and intensive intervention, the majority of children rarely catch up.

The Number of Children Affected

Up to 20 percent of America's children have substantial difficulty learning to read (that could mean more than 10 million children).

Gender Differences

Boys have learning disabilities in only slightly larger numbers than girls, but their problems are far more readily identified because of their more active and boisterous behavior.

Coexisting Problems

About half the young adults with criminal records or a history of substance abuse have reading difficulties.

Phonics

Intervention programs with systematic and explicit instruction in phonics are best. Guided reading aloud is effective (to help with comprehension), and so is instruction in vocabulary and spelling rules.

To find out more, you can get a free written copy of the 40-page summary or 20-minute video from the NICHD. Call 1-800-370-2943 or see www.nationalreadingpanel.org. There are lots of excerpts online at www.ldonline.com (Coordinated Campaign for Learning Disabilities) and www.nrrf.org (National Right to Read Foundation). Search for Reid Lyon.

OTHER REFERENCES

Introduction

- "Boys score lower on reading tests
- Struggling boys act up in class
- Half the young adults involved with crime and drugs (mostly boys) can't read well

Phillips, Gary W.: *The Release of the National Assessment of Educational Progress (NAEP) Fourth-Grade Reading 2000*, National Center for Education Statistics, Apr. 6, 2001, Washington, DC. In 2000, 37 percent of fourth-graders, mostly boys, were below basic reading achievement levels. The literacy gap between boys and girls increased from 1998 to 2000. www.nces.ed.gov.

Galley, Michelle: "Research: Boys to Men," *Education Week*, Jan. 23, 2002. Up to two-thirds of the students who receive special education are boys. The gender gap occurs internationally. School classes don't meet boys' greater need for movement and activity. www.edweek.org.

Riordan, Cornelius: "The Silent Gender Gap," *Education Week*, Nov. 17, 1999. Currently, boys are less likely than girls to be in an academic (college-preparatory) curriculum, have lower educational and occupational expectations, have lower reading and writing test scores, and expect to complete their schooling at an earlier age. www.edweek.org.

Pollack, William S.: *Real Boys: Rescuing Our Sons from the Myths of Boyhood*, New York: Owl Books, 1999. Boys receive five to ten times more disciplinary action in elementary and middle schools than girls.

Porter, Jessica: "Teens' Risky Behavior Tied to School Troubles," *Education Week*, Dec. 6, 2000. School performance has more bearing on whether students experiment with drugs, weapons, violence, and attempted suicide than does either race or family income. www.edweek.org.

National Center for Learning Disabilities (NCLD): *LD Fast Facts*. Between 50 and 60 percent of adolescents in treatment for substance abuse have learning disabilities. www. ld.org.

National Center for Education Statistics (NCES). Male high school students are between four and five times more likely than females to carry a weapon; they are more likely than females to have used alcohol; they are more likely than females to have used marijuana; more males than females drop out of high school; and male students score lower in reading proficiency tests. www.nces.ed.gov.

Lyon, G. Reid: *NICHD Research Program in Reading Development, Reading Disorders and Reading Instruction*, National Institute of Child Health and Human Development document for Keys To Successful Learning Summit, May 1999, Washington, DC. For years boys have been identified as having learning disabilities at four times the rate of girls, but new research finds that boys with learning disabilities don't really outnumber girls—it's their behavior that leads them into remedial classes. See www.nrrf.org and www. ld.org (search "boy").

CHAPTER 1: Does Johnny Have a Problem? Page 3

Page 3: "With reading, we can't afford to 'wait a while.'"

In 1999, a survey (the Roper Poll Survey) of 1700 people found that parents don't realize how important it is to act quickly on reading problems. Parents generally waited before getting help for reading problems, and nearly half the parents surveyed waited more than a year. www.ldonline.org.

Page 5: "The single most important influence on Johnny's success in class will be his teacher."

Arndt, Bettina: "Snips, Snails, Puppy Dogs' Tails: Why Boys Are on the Nose," *The Age* (Australia), June 11, 2001, article based on educational research from Flinders University. "There is now 'conclusive evidence' . . . that teacher quality is by far the most important factor in determining academic outcomes for students . . . and at present, it is boys who are most in need of teachers equipped with the knowledge and skills to help them. . . . Boys see their school problems primarily in terms of their relationships with teachers. They believe there are too many 'bad teachers' who 'don't ask,' 'don't listen' and 'don't care.'" www.theage.com.au.

Milburn, Caroline: "Why Boys Think School Is a Dead Loss," *The Age* (Australia), June 11, 2001. Article based on educational research from Flinders University. "Boys believe secondary school is an unpleasant waste of time and their experiences of education are overwhelmingly negative. . . . Boys told researchers that . . . many boys were regularly humiliated by teachers, ridiculed and made to feel it would be in their best interests to leave. . . . The study found the quality of teachers was a key problem for male students." www.theage.com.au.

Page 7: "Good teachers . . . allow . . . movement."

Galley, Michelle: "Research: Boys to Men," *Education Week*, Jan. 23, 2002. www.edweek.org.

Page 10: "dysgraphia"

Dysgraphia is one of the many *dys* terms we hear nowadays. The prefix *dys* means "difficulty with." Dysgraphia is difficulty with manual handwriting; dyscalculia is difficulty with math. If you want to read more about helping with writing, www.ldonline.com has articles. Search for Writing.

CHAPTER 2: Focusing on Practical Help, Page 13

Page 15: "One in three children is a year or more behind in school."

The Children's Health Council. www.chconline.org.

Page 16: "Dyslexia Facts"

Helmuth, L: "Dyslexia: Same Brains, Different Languages," *Science*, vol. 291, no. 5511, pp. 2035–2262, Mar. 16, 2001.

The National Institute of Mental Health (NIMH) says that brain imaging studies find atypical brain activity in dyslexics, July 3, 1996, release. www.nimh.nih.gov.

On Oct. 6, 1999, the University of Washington released similar findings. www.cac.washington.edu.

The National Institute of Neurological Disorders and Stroke (NINDS), review Oct. 12, 2001. Dyslexia is a brain-based type of learning disability, www.ninds.nih.gov. Dr. Patrick Groff of the NRRF (National Right to Read Foundation) argues an opposite view. He says the biggest factor in whether or not Johnny has dyslexia is his education. Poor teaching is crucial; Johnny must be taught phonics in a structured and systematic way. www.nrrf.org.

CHAPTER 3: How Do I Recognize a Good School? Page 21

Page 23: "If the program is offered by volunteers or peers, the option is still a good one."

Rimm-Kaufman, Sara E., Jerome Kagan, and Happie Byers: "The Effectiveness of Adult Volunteer Tutoring on Reading among 'At Risk' First Grade Children," *Reading Research and Instruction*, vol. 38, no. 2, pp. 143–152, 1999. This study showed excellence in volunteer-run tutoring. Students in a tutoring group met one-on-one with a trained community volunteer who tutored the child three times a week for 45 minutes each session. Students who were tutored read measurably better than those who weren't.

Many articles and books document the advantages of peer mentoring or tutoring. When schools run such programs properly, they spend little money and get great returns. Benard, Bonnie 1990. *A Case For Peers*. Portland, OR: Northwest Regional Educational Laboratory. ED 327 755, 2000. Kalkowski, Page, *Peer and Cross Age Tutoring*. Northwest Regional Educational Laboratory, 1995, Close-up #18.

CHAPTER 5: Do I Need to Get Outside Help? Page 45

Page 48: "Who gives help"

For individual tutors, contact the therapist (www.aetonline.org), consultant (www.educationalconsulting.org), or tutoring agencies (www.professionaltutors.com) listed in the "Web Sites" section. Of the learning centers, Score (www.escore.com), Kumon (www.kumon.com), and Sylvan (www.educate.com) are big. Score centers offer young instructors, computer-assisted instruction, and a reward system that uses shots in basketball hoops. Kumon centers give children worksheets, and a trained Kumon teacher marks and upgrades each child's sheets at every session. At Sylvan centers, children are instructed by qualified schoolteachers and use a progress system that includes spending points at a Sylvan shop.

Page 48: "Does he like a formal or an informal classroom, computers or personal attention, working with a group or alone?"

"Focus: What Was That Project Follow Through?" *Effective School Practices*, vol. 15, no. 1, winter 1995–1996. In "Project Follow Through," the largest educational study every conducted (it went from 1967 to 1995, involved over 15,000 students, and cost over $500 million), the U.S. Department of Education compared different styles of teaching. "Direct instruction," where a teacher directly teaches students and is considered responsible for their learning, was most effective. www.darkwing.uoregon.edu.

CHAPTER 6: Tutoring Johnny Yourself: What to Teach, Page 53

Page 53: "We are able to retrieve only five to nine items from short term memory."

Zimbardo, P., and F. Ruch: *Psychology and Life*, Glenview, Ill.: Scott, Foresman, 1976, p. 154. Short-term memory is used to remember limited amounts of information that we have just learned for very short periods of time. The classic example of short-term memory is remembering telephone numbers. Long-term memory is more permanent, theoretically unlimited in capacity, but less accessible. We need cues or other memory aids (mnemonics, rhymes, or associations) to retrieve it.

Page 57: "When Johnny instantly identifies the frequently occurring words, his reading fluency increases dramatically."

Hall, S., and L. Moats: *Parenting a Struggling Reader,* New York, Broadway Books, 2002, pp. 27–28, 50. Skilled readers learn to recognize common words and letter clusters instantly. To become good readers, they sound out words and word parts, and develop instant recognition of common words and letter patterns.

Page 59: "The Word Folder"

I am grateful to the Ministry of Education in Western Australia for its "First Steps" program. I attended a workshop on First Steps in the early 1990s and was shown excellent strategies and teaching aids. The word folder was inspired by the First Steps Spelling Journal.

Page 91: "Reading Facts"

Telford, Lesley: "A Study of Boys' Reading," *Early Child Development and Care*, vol. 149, pp. 87–124, February 1999. Boys are more confident reading at home, where they don't feel the need to cover up perceived low ability. Parents and family members can provide important role modeling and support.

Vadon, Albert M.: *Gender and Cultural Differences in Attitude toward Reading in an Adult Population*, M.A. Research Project, Kean University, 2000. We may unintentionally give boys unhelpful messages about reading. This study found that both men and women viewed reading as a mostly feminine activity.

The National Literacy Trust: "Attitudes toward reading," a MORI (Market and Opinion Research International) social research study on behalf of the National Literacy Trust, September 1998. Younger people (those under 25) have the least positive attitudes toward reading. Young men in particular appeared to dislike reading, but also claimed that they would read books about subjects that interested them. www.literacytrust.org.uk.

Andre, Thomas, Myrna Whigham, Amy Hendrickson, and Sharon Chambers: "Science and Mathematics versus Other School Subject Areas: Pupil Attitudes versus Parent Attitudes," paper presented at the Annual Meeting of the National Association for Research in Science Teaching, Chicago, March 1997. Girls perceived themselves as being better at reading, while boys thought of themselves as being better at physical science. Parents shared the same perceptions of boys' competencies.

Simpson, Anne: "Fictions and Facts: An Investigation of the Reading Practices of Girls and Boys," *English Education*, vol. 28, no. 4, pp. 268–279, December 1996. Boys read far less than girls, but over more genres.

CHAPTER 7: Tutoring Johnny Yourself: How to Teach, Page 99

Page 101: "multisensory techniques"

For more information, see www.surfaquarium.com and www.ldpride.net.

Chapter 8: Homework, Page 115

Page 116: "The average child watches over 3 hours of TV every day"

California elementary schools information sheet to parents, Apr. 23–29, 2001, from the TV-Turnoff Network, www.tvturnoff.org.

Page 116: " students with learning disabilities engaged in practices that interfered with homework completion to a greater extent than other children."

Gajria, Meenakshi, and Spencer J. Salend: "Homework Practices of Students with and without Learning Disabilities: A Comparison," *Journal of Learning Disabilities*, vol. 28, no. 5, pp. 291–296, May 1995.

Page 116: "A child's ability to ignore visual distractions and get work done depends on 'the availability of working memory.'"

de Fockert, J. W., G. Rees, C. D. Frith, and N. Lavie: "The Role of Working Memory in Visual Selective Attention," *Science*, vol. 291, no. 5509, Mar. 2, 2001.

Page 117: "kids these days do much more sophisticated homework than we did"

Sites that can help Johnny find information for reports are: www.ajkids.com, www.google.com, and www.yahooligans.com.

Page 117: "a lot is at stake"

Ratnesar, Romesh, et al.: "The Homework Ate My Family," *Time*, vol. 153, no. 3, pp. 54–63, Jan. 25, 1999. This study confirms what many parents fear. Homework can have many harmful effects because it eats up family time and causes stress and unhappiness.

Chapter 9: Boy Issues, Page 125

Page 125: "Boys have learning disabilities in slightly larger numbers than girls but are identified as having learning disabilities about three times as often because of their more boisterous behavior."

NCLD. www.ld.org.

Galley, Michelle: "Research: Boys to Men," *Education Week*, Jan. 23, 2002. About 20 percent of boys referred for special education are referred by regular teachers because of their behavior. Only 2.5 percent of girls referred for special education get there because of their behavior. www.edweek.org.

Page 127: "consistently produced only one or two muddled sentences each lesson"

To read articles about writing, visit www.ldonline.org and search for Writing.

Page 130: "The Self-Fulfilling Prophecy"

Zimbardo, P., and F. Ruch: *Psychology and Life*, Glenview, Ill.: Scott Foresman, 1976.

Meyenn, Bob, Judith Parker, and Katie Maher: "Come Along Then the Naughty Boys; Perspectives on Boys and Discipline," paper presented at the Annual Meeting of the American Educational Research Association, San Diego, Calif., April 13–17, 1998. Describes how teachers stereotype boys' behavior.

Didham, Cheryl K.: "Equal Opportunity in the Classroom— Making Teachers Aware," paper presented at the Annual Meeting of the Association of Teacher Educators, Las Vegas, Nev., Feb. 5–8, 1990.

Page 131: "ADHD"

Schwab Learning Center, 2002, article by Kristin Stanberry. Hyperactivity and impulsive behaviors are the key traits that get so many boys referred for ADHD testing. Some studies estimate that six times as many boys as girls are referred. Recent studies suggest the actual ratio of boys to girls is 3 to 1 and that boys' wilder behavior just gets them noticed so much more than girls. See also www.docdiller.com.

Page 132: "Dad Deficiency Disorder"

Biddulph, Steve: *Raising Boys*, Berkeley, Calif.: Celestial Arts, 1998, p. 21.

Chapter 10: Guiding Johnny's Behavior, Page 137

Page 146: "If consequences bother you, you can do without them."

Wolf, Anthony E.: *The Secret of Parenting*, New York: Farrar, Straus & Giroux, 2000.
10 Quickest and Best Tips

Top 10 Quickest and Best Tips, Page 167

Page 169: "Computers"

Torgesen, Joe: "Hooked on Phonics." Dr. Torgesen of the Florida State University believes that instruction in phonics is valuable, even if it's from CDs like Hooked on Phonics, but that gains from personal tutoring are greatest. Whether it's with an older child or an adult, person-to-person contact makes all the difference. www.research.fsu.edu.

Index

About the Author

Tracey Wood, mom and children's reading specialist, holds a Bachelor of Education (Honors) degree in Education and Psychology, a Diploma in Special Education and a Master's degree in Education. She is a member of the Learning Disabilities Association of America (LDA), the Council for Learning Disabilities (CLD), and the California Reading Association. Tracey has helped struggling children and their parents for over 18 years, working in England and Australia before settling in America. Until recently Tracey ran a reading and writing clinic in the San Francisco Bay Area, where she also helped at her children's school, led two scouting troops, and instructed for the Red Cross. She now lives in Toronto and can be contacted through her web site www.readingpains.com.